A VEGETARIAN IN THE FAMILY

Shows how the lone vegetarian can co-exist without mealtime problems. The recipes given are not only for individual meals, but also include 'spin-offs' from the rest of the family's meat dishes.

A VEGETARIAN IN THE FAMILY

by

JANET HUNT

Illustrated by Ian Jones

THORSONS PUBLISHING GROUP

Produced in co-operation with
The Vegetarian Society of the United Kingdom Ltd.
Parkdale, Dunham Road, Altrincham, Cheshire

First published 1977
Second Edition, revised, expanded and reset, 1984

© JANET HUNT 1984

British Library Cataloguing in Publication Data

Hunt, Janet,
A vegetarian in the family.—2nd ed.
1. Vegetarian cookery
I. Title
641.5'636   TX837

ISBN 0-7225-0900-6

*Published by Thorsons Publishers Limited,
Wellingborough, Northamptonshire, NN8 2RQ, England*

Printed in Great Britain by Richard Clay Limited,
Bungay, Suffolk

7 9 11 13 15 16 14 12 10 8

CONTENTS

1.

FIRST THINGS FIRST

A vegetarian in a family of meat-eaters usually gets a rough deal. All too often his or her meals consist of what everyone else is having, minus the meat. And a plate of potatoes and two vegetables not only becomes boring when repeated daily — but can be positively dangerous.

Everyone needs a variety of nutrients to build and maintain the kind of health that makes life a joyful experience. Meat is a prime source of protein, and when it is dropped from the diet, that essential protein must be obtained from elsewhere. Although potatoes and vegetables do supply it, the amount is minimal, but a boost can be given by the simple addition of such ingredients as nuts, seeds, cheese, eggs, lentils, beans, soya flour and dried milk powder. However, replacing the protein on your plate is only part of the story.

The value of a balanced diet is receiving an increasing amount of publicity in the press, on TV and radio — and in the doctor's surgery, too. Foods that have long been accepted as part of the conventional diet are becoming suspect, and health foods are no longer regarded as cranky. For the vegetarian, a balanced diet means avoiding denatured and devitalized foods like white flour, white sugar, white rice, and eating instead wholewheat bread and cakes, raw brown sugar or honey, and brown unpolished rice. It means cutting down on excessive fats, and cutting out completely foodstuffs that are full of chemicals, colouring, preservatives and flavouring. It means eating more crisp, fresh salads; sweet and juicy fruits; vegetables cooked only briefly so as to retain their goodness. It means, in short, going back to the simple diet our bodies thrive on.

One excuse frequently given for not following such a diet is that, although it consists of very basic foods, many of them are only available from health food shops at prices that are anything but basic! This is not entirely true as many supermarkets are now catching on, and catering for a growing demand for foods that build health. And many of the items they do not as yet supply can be bought at health food shops at prices that seem ridiculously low when compared with the price of meat protein. Pulses, wholewheat cereals, eggs, tvp, all are excellent ways of filling your stomach and your body's requirements without emptying your purse.

Working Together
Once you have decided to be vegetarian, dropping meat from your diet is not at all difficult, but sharing your life and kitchen with a family who still eat meat *can* cause problems. But such problems are not insurmountable, and you should not let them put you off. All it takes is a little bit of organizing with regard to cupboard space, use of kitchen work surfaces and cooker; some forethought and co-operation so that you can still enjoy your meals together as a family; and a genuine desire to understand each other's point of view. Besides, nowadays the high price of meat is forcing many dedicated meat-eaters to eat vegetarian at least a couple of times a week, so you may well find yourself sharing your meatless meal.

Most of the utensils necessary to cook varied and interesting meals will already be part of the kitchen equipment. A grinder/blender for milling nuts, liquidizing vegetables for delicious soups or fruit for drinks; a good grater for grating cheese, and bread to make breadcrumbs; a wooden spoon for lump-free sauces; a steamer for cooking vegetables. All very useful items for vegetarian and meat-eater alike. An expensive but invaluable extra is a pressure cooker which will save an enormous amount of time, especially when cooking bean dishes, and which can be used to make thick soups, meals-in-one-pot, and all sorts of concoctions.

Shopping needn't be a daily event for the vegetarian because many of the foods that form the basis of the meatless diet can be stored, if not indefinitely, then certainly for long periods of time. These are the true convenience foods; not adulterated apologies for the real thing, but pure foods that simply need hydrating or milling or soaking before cooking, and are ready in no time. What's more, they usually take only a small amount of space. It's a good idea to keep a separate cupboard or section of a cupboard for vegetarian items so that they can be found and reached with ease.

Fresh Foods

There are some foods, of course, that you will need to buy frequently. Vegetables and fruit, for example, need to be fresh if you are going to obtain the maximum nutrients from them. You can keep costs down when buying at the greengrocer's by choosing seasonal produce — you will find they taste best, too. Be adventurous with vegetables and try some of the more unfamiliar items. Nowadays there is a huge variety to choose from, and they will brighten up your meals considerably. There is no reason why they should not be served to the rest of the family, either.

Bread is best bought fresh in small amounts, though you can always use up any extra as toast, or make it into crumbs and store them in a screw-top jar in the fridge. (If you make your own bread, you need never have to run out again!) Cheeses will keep a little longer, though the fresher they are, the better they'll taste. Again, any leftover cheese can be grated and kept ready for instant use in a cooked dish. Although most hard cheeses are made with animal rennet, a number of vegetarian cheeses are now available, and many of the softer cheeses are made without the use of rennet of any kind.

Other ingredients to keep in your store cupboard in *small* amounts are free-range eggs, tofu, nut butters and nuts. How long they will keep depends on how fresh they were when you bought them, so it's worth going to a reliable store, preferably one with a brisk business and fast turnover of stock.

In this book I give enough recipes to keep you going until you have mastered the art of vegetarian cookery — for have no doubts about it, you will have to learn to approach your meals in a completely new way. Be prepared at first to devote a little more time to your cookery as new methods and strange ingredients take some getting used to! If you can manage ten minutes once a week to plan your menus for the next seven days, you will save both time and effort, *and* enjoy your food more. Eventually you will want to try swapping one ingredient for another, adding something completely different, maybe even inventing new dishes of your own. In this way vegetarian cookery becomes fun as well as being a compassionate, inexpensive and satisfying way of eating. Who knows, you may convince the rest of the family that it is worth a try.

Veganism

If your decision to become vegetarian was based on a desire to help alleviate animal suffering, the logical conclusion is to become a vegan. Some strong-willed individuals, once aware of the suffering involved not just with the production of meat, but with milk, cheese and eggs too, switch overnight from being meat-eaters to being vegans. Although there is no reason why you should not do this, it is more usual — and maybe more sensible — to become a vegetarian at least for a short time first. This enables your body to adjust to new foods, and your mind to learn both new techniques of cookery and new combinations of ingredients.

Although vegetarians are now widely accepted in this country, vegans are still tainted with the image of cranks. (In fact, they have taken the place of vegetarians in the society of 50 years ago!) No doubt time will correct this. Already the medical profession are realizing that the vegan diet — rich in fruit and vegetables, grains and nuts — is a very healthy one. Meanwhile, if you intend to be a vegan in a family of meat-eaters, follow the advice already given for vegetarians. Be firm but do not preach, be adaptable within the rules you have set yourself and try to eat as often as possible with the rest of the family so that you are still one of them. However, the most important thing you must do is read up as much as possible about nutrition, so that you are equipped with at least a basic knowledge about what your body needs to be healthy. Because the vegan diet is restricted it *can* lead to a variety of problems, though this need not happen if you know your onions! Learn what is what, and even if your family start out doubting the wisdom of your new way of eating, you'll prove to them that you know exactly what you are doing.

One last point — many of the recipes here are for one person, but those that are more fiddly, or difficult to cook in small amounts, are usually for two. If you are the only one in the family who will be eating this particular dish, you will probably find that any leftovers will keep well in the fridge for a few days; longer still in the freezer.

2.

SUNSHINE BREAKFASTS

A real sunshine breakfast is more than just a puff of wheat sprinkled with sugar and drowned in milk. It's a mini-meal super-charged with protein, vitamins and other good things to get you going after a night's rest, and keep you going through the busiest day.

Of course you want to eat breakfast with the rest of the family, and there is no reason why you shouldn't. If the traditional English breakfast is popular with your nearest and dearest, you too can have cereal, fried eggs with mushrooms and tomato, toast, marmalade, coffee. For an especially nutritious version just make sure the cereal and toast are wholegrain, and that you fry your eggs — preferably free-range — in a polyunsaturated vegetable oil such as corn or sunflower (better still, poach or scramble them).

If the mere thought of all that food so early in the day is enough to upset your stomach, try some of the many alternative breakfasts that give just as much nourishment for far less effort. A high protein breakfast-in-a-glass; the increasingly popular muesli with fresh or dried fruit; wholewheat toast and peanut butter. Nutrition experts agree that breakfast is the most important meal of the day, so it's worth experimenting until you find the one that gets your day off to the brightest start.

Note: Unless otherwise stated the recipes given throughout this book are for one person only.

Cereals, Nuts and Fruit

MUESLI

Imperial (Metric)
1 tablespoonful oatmeal or oat flakes
¼ pint (140ml) milk
1 large apple
1 tablespoonful ground nuts
1 tablespoonful thin honey
Juice of ½ lemon
Soft seasonal or dried fruits

American
1 tablespoonful oatmeal or oat flakes
⅔ cupful milk
1 large apple
1 tablespoonful ground nuts
1 tablespoonful thin honey
Juice of ½ lemon
Soft seasonal or dried fruits

1. When using oatmeal, soak it overnight in 2 tablespoonsful of water. (Oat flakes can be used unsoaked).

2. Mix the oats and milk, grate the apple finely and add.

3. Now stir in all the other ingredients and, if you like your food to look attractive, garnish with some of the fruit. Eat at once.

Note: The variations that can be made to this basic muesli recipe are endless. You can use a mixed cereal base with wheat, millet and/or barley flakes. For a crunchy texture carefully toast some of the flakes under the grill for a few minutes. Ground nuts can be replaced with broken or whole nuts or seeds, honey with raw brown sugar. Slimmers can use skimmed milk or yogurt, the underweight can indulge with single cream.

CRUNCHY GRANOLA

Imperial (Metric)	American
3 tablespoonsful vegetable oil	3 tablespoonsful vegetable oil
½ lb (225g) thin honey	¾ cupful thin honey
1 tablespoonful vanilla (optional)	1 tablespoonful vanilla (optional)
1 lb (455g) rolled oats	4 cupsful rolled oats
4 oz (115g) mixed chopped nuts	¾ cupful mixed chopped nuts
4 oz (115g) sunflower seeds	¾ cupful sunflower seeds
4 oz (115g) wheatgerm	1 cupful wheatgerm
4 oz (115g) sesame seeds	¾ cupful sesame seeds
Dried fruits — various	Dried fruits — various

1. Heat the oil, honey and vanilla gently in a large pan then add the oats, stirring them until all are covered with the honey mixture.

2. When the oats turn light gold, add the nuts and sunflower seeds, stir well, and continue cooking on a low heat for 5-10 minutes.

3. Then add the wheatgerm and sesame seeds and continue cooking and stirring until the granola is a rich brown.

4. Turn off heat, cool, and add the dried fruit.

Note: This healthy, crunchy American-style breakfast can be stored in an airtight container and used as needed. It's very satisfying so the amount given here will last for ages. Granola is usually eaten with milk or yogurt, but try it as a desert with cream or use it as a topping for fruit crumble. You will find it very versatile.

CINNAMON PORRIDGE

Imperial (Metric)
2 oz (55g) rolled oats
Approx. 6 tablespoonsful water
1 teaspoonful cinnamon, or to taste
Pinch of sea salt
1 oz (30g) raw cane sugar, or to taste
Milk or cream
½ dessert apple (optional)

American
½ cupful rolled oats
½ cupful water
1 teaspoonful cinnamon, or to taste
Pinch of sea salt
2 tablespoonsful raw cane sugar, or to taste
Milk or cream
½ dessert apple (optional)

1. In a small, heavy based saucepan combine the oats, water, cinnamon and salt, and bring them to the boil. Lower the heat and cook gently for about 20 minutes, or until the oats are tender and the liquid has been absorbed.

2. Serve the porridge sweetened to taste, and topped with a little milk or cream. Grated apple stirred into the dish is delicious, especially if topped with a sprinkling more of cinnamon and sugar.

3. This porridge is fairly firm in texture. If you prefer a more liquid consistency, adjust the water or add more milk. You can also make up more than you need, and use the extra for tomorrow's breakfast.

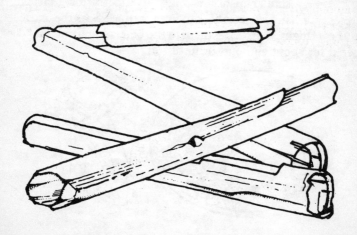

SUMMER WHEAT GRAIN BREAKFAST

Imperial (Metric)	American
1 tablespoonful cooked wheat grain	1 tablespoonful cooked wheat grain
1 tablespoonful oatmeal or oat flakes	1 tablespoonful oatmeal or oat flakes
Approx. ¼ pint (140ml) milk	⅔ cupful milk
1 oz (30g) raisins	2 tablespoonsful raisins
1 tablespoonful honey, or to taste	1 tablespoonful honey, or to taste
Soft fruit in season	Soft fruit in season

1. The ideal time to make this dish is when you have some leftover wheat grains to use up. Drain the wheat grains well, tip them into a bowl, and stir in the oatmeal and enough milk to give a porridge-like consistency.

2. Stir in the raisins, sweeten to taste, and sprinkle with a spoonful or two of soft fruits such as blackberries, raspberries or strawberries. The firm texture of the wheat grains, the creaminess of the oats, and the strongly flavoured fruits go deliciously well together.

3. You can turn this into a winter breakfast by serving it with hot milk, and using chopped or grated apples or pears instead of the soft fruit.

Note: A very similar dish you might like to try for a change is Frumenty, a dish that dates back to Roman times. Soak the uncooked grains overnight, then bring them to the boil, add raisins, and cook covered for about an hour, or until soft.

FRUIT AND NUT BREAKFAST

For each person:

1-2 tablespoonsful dried fruit
1-2 tablespoonsful oat flakes
1-2 tablespoonsful ground nuts

1. Chop larger fruit like apricots, then soak all the fruit overnight in just enough water to cover it.

2. Mix the oats and nuts and sprinkle over the fruit before serving.

FRUIT COMPOTE

Wash dried fruit then soak overnight in just enough warm water to cover it. A few drops of lemon juice bring out the true fruit flavour and you can add a little honey if you've a sweet tooth. Only simmer the fruit if you want it extra soft. Prepare enough for two days or so at a time as it keeps well in the fridge — some say the flavour even improves. Use combinations of such fruits as apricots, sliced dried bananas, currants, dates, prunes, raisins, sultanas, figs. Dried fruits are rich in iron and should be eaten often, especially if you have been used to obtaining much of your iron from meat.

Breakfasts in a Glass

EGG-FRUIT FLIP

For each person:

2 teaspoonsful thin honey
1 egg
Juice of 1 lemon
Juice of 1 orange

1. Whisk the honey into the egg, strain, and add the fruit juices.

2. For a change vary one or both of the fruits using fresh, bottled, frozen or tinned juice, i.e. blackcurrant, apple, peach, pear, pineapple.

BLACKCURRANT-YOGURT DRINK

For each person:

½ glassful blackcurrant juice
½ glassful plain unsweetened yogurt

1. Add the fruit juice to the yogurt and whisk until light and frothy.

2. Again you can completely change the taste of this drink by varying the fruits. (Apple is delicious with a pinch of cinnamon).

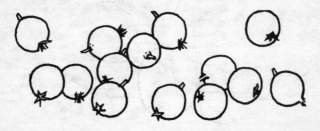

NUT MILK

A particularly protein-packed breakfast-in-a-glass is made by combining ground nuts with fruit juice. Good combinations are cashew or almond/orange juice; walnut/grapefruit juice; hazelnuts/pineapple juice. You can also use sunflower or sesame seeds. For all these recipes a hand whisk will do, but an electric blender does the job quicker and more thoroughly.

CREAMY TOFU SHAKE

Imperial (Metric)
3 oz (85g) tofu
⅓ pint (200ml) orange juice, fresh or frozen
Maple syrup or honey to taste

American
½ cupful tofu
¾ cupful orange juice, fresh or frozen
Maple syrup or honey to taste

1. Press the tofu gently but firmly to remove any excess moisture — it helps if you wrap it first in a clean cloth. Cut it into cubes and put it into a blender with the orange juice and sweetening.

2. Purée until thick and smooth, then chill lightly before drinking your tofu shake.

3. You can, of course, use a variety of different fruit juices in this breakfast drink, either fresh or frozen. Raw cane sugar, preferably ground to a powder first, can also be used, though the honey or maple syrup give a more interesting flavour. If you prefer a more liquid consistency, adjust the amount of fruit juice accordingly.

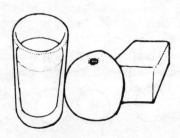

The Fried Breakfast

Throughout the world, Britain is famous for its fried breakfast, a dish that usually consists of fried sausages and kidneys, vegetables, eggs and bread. Although high in protein, it's not a good breakfast as fried food is particularly difficult to digest, so the stomach is rudely awakened from a night's rest with an excess of work to do. This often accounts not only for cases of chronic indigestion, but also helps explain why some people find their early morning doziness can continue until midday!

As an occasional treat, however, a fried breakfast makes a pleasant change, and if your family are having a fry-up you can have most of the things they have. Using pure vegetable oils such as peanut, corn or sunflower helps you digest your fried food — in fact, everyone in the family should be encouraged to use such polyunsaturated oils. Fry food for the minimum period necessary, don't have the heat too high, and always drain fried food on a paper towel before eating it.

FRIED BREAKFAST
Serves 4

Imperial (Metric)	American
8 small Potato Cakes (see page 22)	8 small Potato Cakes (see page 22)
Small tin soya 'sausages'	Small can soy 'sausages'
4 oz (115g) mushrooms	2 cupsful mushrooms
8 medium tomatoes	8 medium tomatoes
4 eggs	4 eggs
Vegetable oil for frying	Vegetable oil for frying
Parsley for garnish (optional)	Parsley for garnish (optional)

1. Make the potato cakes first — preferably the night before. Drain and pat dry the soya sausages. Slice the cleaned mushrooms, wash and halve the tomatoes.

2. Heat some oil in a large frying pan and first cook the Potato Cakes (see page 22). Drain them well and then put aside in the warm, an ideal spot being the oven with the heat set at its lowest.

3. Lightly fry the 'sausages', turning them frequently so that they colour evenly. Put them with the potato cakes.

4. Add a little more oil to the pan if necessary, then lightly fry the sliced mushrooms. If there is room in the pan, cook the tomatoes at the same time. Keep these items warm whilst you fry the eggs for the minimum time — over-cooked eggs will be tough and tasteless.

5. Serve at once. A garnish of fresh parsley looks attractive.

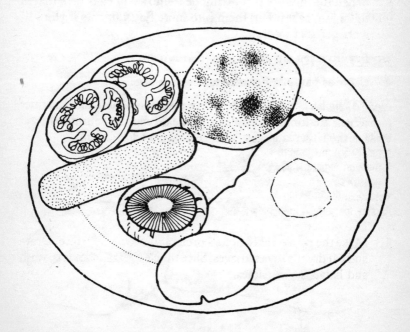

POTATO CAKES
Serves 4

Imperial (Metric)	American
1 lb (455g) potatoes	1 pound potatoes
1 small onion	1 small onion
1 egg	1 egg
2 oz (55g) plain wholemeal flour	½ cupful plain wholewheat flour
Good pinch of marjoram	Good pinch of marjoram
Seasoning to taste	Seasoning to taste
Flour or oats for coating	Flour or oats for coating
Vegetable oil for frying	Vegetable oil for frying

1. Peel and boil or steam the potatoes until soft enough to mash. Cutting them into cubes makes this quicker — using leftovers is easier still! Add the finely chopped onion, beaten egg, flour, herbs and seasoning.

2. When the mixture is cool, divide it into small balls then flatten them into cakes. Dip them into more flour, or oats if you like a crisper coating.

3. Fry in vegetable oil until golden brown.

4. Serve as part of a Fried Breakfast (see page 20).

Note: As such a breakfast is likely to be a social occasion, the quantities given here are for four people. The meat-eaters in your family can replace the soya 'sausages' with real ones and/or bacon.

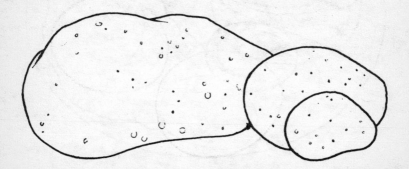

Egg Dishes

Most vegetarians use only free-range eggs as they have not been produced under cruel 'factory' conditions, and are also more wholesome and tasty. Make sure the eggs you buy are fresh by checking that the shell is dull. A shiny shell indicates the egg has been around long enough to have lost that natural matt look — and maybe some of its goodness too.

BAKED EGGS

Butter a ramekin dish or heatproof saucer (use a larger dish if cooking more eggs) then break an egg into it, season, and cover with the top of the milk or thin cream. Cook at the bottom of a medium oven 350°F/180°C (Gas Mark 4) standing in a tray of water until just set. An ideal dish when you are using the oven to make hot rolls for weekend breakfasts.

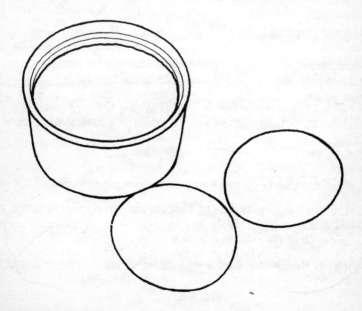

LUXURY SCRAMBLED EGGS

For each person:

2 eggs
2 tablespoonsful cream
Pinch of sea salt

1. Whisk the ingredients together thoroughly.

2. Heat a knob of butter in a heavy pan, pour in the eggs and cook gently, continually stirring up the cooked eggs on the bottom of the pan.

3. As the mixture starts to thicken turn the heat even lower and remove eggs from heat the moment they reach the desired consistency.

4. Grated onion, sautéed chopped mushrooms, minced parsley or a spoonful of wheatgerm can be added if liked.

FRENCH TOAST

Imperial (Metric)	American
1 tablespoonful milk	1 tablespoonful milk
1 egg	1 egg
Sea salt and freshly ground pepper	Sea salt and freshly ground pepper
3 slices lightly buttered wholemeal bread	3 slices lightly buttered wholewheat bread
Vegetable oil	Vegetable oil

1. Beat milk and egg together. Add seasoning as required.

2. Dip the bread into the egg mixture and drop quickly into hot oil in a frying pan. Only fry the bread for a minute, then turn it over and fry the other side.

3. Drain, then put on a plate with whatever you fancy — a savoury

topping like grilled mushrooms or tomatoes, or a dribbling of mild honey. If you like bananas, slice one on to your French toast and then add some honey and a sprinkling of chopped nuts.

Note: This is a very filling dish so you may like to share it with someone else in the family. What nicer way to start a lazy Sunday or brighten up a dreary Monday!

CHILLI EGGS À LA MODE
Serves 2

Imperial (Metric)	American
3 medium tomatoes	3 medium tomatoes
2 teaspoonsful vegetable oil	2 teaspoonsful vegetable oil
Pinch of chilli powder to taste	Pinch of chili powder to taste
2 thick slices wholemeal bread	2 thick slices wholewheat bread
Polyunsaturated margarine or butter	Polyunsaturated margarine or butter
2 eggs	2 eggs
Parsley to garnish	Parsley to garnish

1. Wash and then chop the tomatoes. Heat the oil and sauté the tomatoes for 5 minutes, stirring frequently. Then add the chilli powder and a few spoonsful of water, and cook gently until completely softened.

2. Toast the bread and spread lightly with margarine. At the same time boil the eggs for just 2 minutes. Remove the shells without breaking the eggs and place one on each slice of toast.

3. Top with a generous portion of the hot tomatoes, sprinkle with parsley, and your breakfast is ready.

4. As this is a rather fiddly breakfast recipe, the quantities given are for two on the assumption that someone may share it with you. If either of you find the thought of chilli for breakfast rather daunting, dilute the taste (without ruining the effect) by stirring a spoonful or two of plain yogurt or tahini into the tomatoes just before serving.

Waffles

Here is another popular American breakfast dish fast catching on in this country. They are easy to make, delicious to eat, and if you make more than you need on a morning when you have some extra time in hand, you can freeze those you don't eat, or just put them in the fridge. They will make a quick breakfast or snack during the week — just warm them briefly on a medium heat in the oven.

WAFFLES

Imperial (Metric)	American
4 oz (115g) wholemeal flour	1 cupful wholewheat flour
Pinch of sea salt	Pinch of sea salt
1 egg	1 egg
⅓ pint (200ml) milk	¾ cupful milk
1 oz (30g) melted polyunsaturated margarine	2½ tablespoonsful melted polyunsaturated margarine
1 oz (30g) raw cane sugar	2 tablespoonsful raw cane sugar

1. Sift flour and salt into a bowl, make a well in the centre and drop in the egg.

2. Beat thoroughly then gradually add the milk, beating all the time so that you have a really smooth batter.

3. Add the melted margarine and sugar.

4. Grease the waffle iron, heat for 2-3 minutes, then pour in just enough of the batter to cover it. Close the waffle iron for 2 minutes and the waffle should be crisp, brown and ready to eat with molasses, melted butter, jam, cream, or the traditional maple syrup.

Note: Waffle irons can be brought at good ironmongers and most department stores.

3.

SOUPS, SALADS AND
SANDWICHES

A soup can be whatever you wish: cold or hot; light and appetizing; or a complete meal in itself. It's a tasty way to serve up leftovers, and if you use stock from cooked vegetables as the base you have the added goodness of all those vitamins. You may ask: 'Why should I bother to make my own when there are so many instant soups available?' If the list of ingredients doesn't answer this question, the flavour certainly will!

Sadly, salads are often dismissed by gourmets as 'rabbit food'. Even worse, they frequently deserve the title! Yet so many things can be added to the usual greenery to make a feast for the eyes and the taste buds. Vegetables like endive, cauliflower, leeks, fennel, asparagus, sweetcorn, fresh and dried fruits, avocado, nuts, ginger, seeds. If you can eat it, add it to your salad! Top it with a tasty dressing, and you'll find everyone in the family will want to try it (they can always add some cold meat or fish, if they must).

Everyone eats sandwiches. They are quick and easy — but they can be boring. Try the fillings suggested here, then invent some of your own. Wholewheat bread sandwiches travel well so if you are out at work you needn't make do with 'empty' foods from the corner café.

Note: Quantities given in this section are for two. If you do not intend to share your soup with another member of the family, pour it into a screw-top jar and store it in the refrigerator for a day or two, to be re-heated when you fancy it — or maybe served chilled?

Soups

RAGGED EGG SOUP

Imperial (Metric)	American
1 egg	1 egg
1 tablespoonful fine wholemeal semolina	1 tablespoonful fine wholewheat semolina
2 tablespoonsful Parmesan cheese	2 tablespoonsful Parmesan cheese
1 pint (570ml) vegetable stock*	2½ cupsful vegetable stock*
Seasoning to taste	Seasoning to taste

1. Beat egg, semolina, cheese and a little of the stock together.

2. Heat remaining stock and when almost boiling pour in the egg mixture, stirring continuously. The egg will cook in little ragged pieces.

3. Allow the soup to come just to boiling point, season as necessary, and serve at once.

Note: This popular Italian soup (its other name is *Stracciatella*) is very tasty and light, yet the egg boosts its food value considerably. Unfortunately it is impossible to make in a smaller amount, and it does not keep well, so persuade another member of the family to share it with you.

* Vegetable stock can be bought in cube form at your local health food store.

PEANUT SOUP

Imperial (Metric)	American
2 oz (55g) smooth peanut butter	1/2 cupful smooth peanut butter
1/2 pint (285ml) vegetable stock	1 1/3 cupsful vegetable stock
1/4 pint (140ml) milk	2/3 cupful milk
1/4 teaspoonful chilli powder	1/4 teaspoonful chilli powder
1/4 teaspoonful sea salt	1/4 teaspoonful sea salt

1. Blend peanut butter with a little of the hot vegetable stock until dissolved, then pour into a saucepan and add all the other ingredients.

2. Bring to the boil, stirring occasionally, then reduce heat and simmer soup for 15 minutes.

3. Serve hot with a dab of whipped cream on top, or cold with thin slices of cucumber.

Note: This is enough for two good bowls of soup and if no-one wants to share it with you, the uneaten portion will keep for a day or so in the refrigerator. Check that the peanut butter you use has the minimum of additives and artificial flavouring — the soup will be that much more tasty.

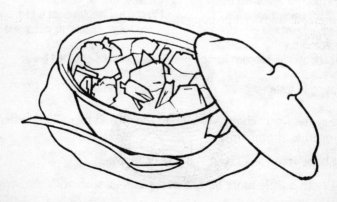

VEGETABLE BROTH

Imperial (Metric)	American
1/2 lb (225g) mixed vegetables, including onion and carrot	1 1/4 cupsful mixed vegetables, including onion and carrot
1 tablespoonsful vegetable oil	1 tablespoonful vegetable oil
1 pint (570ml) vegetable stock or water	2 1/2 cupsful vegetable stock or water
1 teaspoonful yeast extract	1 teaspoonful yeast extract
Seasoning to taste	Seasoning to taste
Chopped parsley, chives, or other fresh herbs	Chopped parsley, chives, or other fresh herbs

1. Chop the vegetables into small pieces and cook in the oil over a gentle heat for a few minutes.

2. Add the stock or water and simmer until the vegetables are just tender.

3. Stir in the yeast extract, season to taste, and serve this soup as it is, or liquidized. Sprinkle chopped herbs on top.

FORCEMEAT DUMPLINGS

Imperial (Metric)	American
1 small onion	1 small onion
1 tablespoonful vegetable oil	1 tablespsoonful vegetable oil
3 oz (85g) wholemeal bread, crumbled, soaked in water and squeezed dry	1 1/2 cupsful wholewheat bread, crumbled, soaked in water and squeezed dry
1 dessertspoonful chopped herbs	2 teaspoonsful chopped herbs
1 egg yolk	1 egg yolk
Seasoning to taste	Seasoning to taste

1. Fry the finely chopped onion in the oil and mix all ingredients together thoroughly.

2. Shape into balls about the size of marbles.

3. Fry in a little more oil and serve as a garnish with the soup.

CORN AND POTATO CHOWDER

Imperial (Metric)	American
½ lb (225g) peeled potatoes, diced into small pieces	1⅓ cupsful peeled potatoes, diced into small pieces
1 chopped onion	1 chopped onion
1 tablespoonful vegetable oil	1 tablespoonful vegetable oil
1 pint (570ml) vegetable stock, or water and milk	2½ cupsful vegetable stock, or water and milk
1 oz (30g) wholemeal flour	4 tablespoonsful wholewheat flour
1 teaspoonful yeast extract	1 teaspoonful yeast extract
1 small tin of sweetcorn	1 small can of sweetcorn
Seasoning to taste	Seasoning to taste
Finely grated carrot and chopped parsley	Finely grated carrot and chopped parsley

1. Cook the potatoes and onion in the oil for a few minutes then add the liquid and simmer until the potatoes are just tender.

2. Cream the flour with some of the liquid from the pan, add the yeast extract and stir into the potato mixture.

3. Cook for a few minutes to thicken, then drain the tin of sweetcorn and add the contents to the soup.

4. Check the seasoning, stir in the carrot and parsley, and serve piping hot. A very filling soup for a cold winter's day.

LENTIL SOUP

Imperial (Metric)
6 oz (170g) rinsed lentils
1 finely chopped onion
1 grated carrot
¾ pint (425ml) vegetable stock or
  water
1 bay leaf and a pinch of mixed
  herbs
1 tablespoonful vegetable oil
1 oz (30g) wholemeal flour
¼ pint (140ml) milk
1 teaspoonful yeast extract
Seasoning to taste

American
¾ cupful rinsed lentils
1 finely chopped onion
1 grated carrot
2 cupsful vegetable stock or water
1 bay leaf and a pinch of mixed
  herbs
1 tablespoonful vegetable oil
4 tablespoonsful wholewheat flour
⅔ cupful milk
1 teaspoonful yeast extract
Seasoning to taste

1. Simmer the lentils, onion and carrot in the stock or water with
   the bay leaf and herbs until the lentils collapse.

2. Make a thin sauce with the oil, flour and milk, add the yeast
   extract.

3. Combine the sauce with the lentil mixture (first removing the
   bay leaf), check the seasoning, and serve the soup as it is, or
   liquidized for a smoother taste.

TOMATO AND LEEK SOUP

Imperial (Metric)
3 medium tomatoes, roughly
  chopped
1 finely chopped leek
1 tablespoonful vegetable oil
1 pint (570ml) vegetable stock, milk
  and water, or water
Seasoning and herbs to taste

American
3 medium tomatoes, roughly
  chopped
1 finely chopped leek
1 tablespoonful vegetable oil
2½ cupsful vegetable stock, milk
  and water, or water
Seasoning and herbs to taste

1. Cook the tomatoes and leek in the oil for a few minutes then add the liquid and simmer until the vegetables are just cooked.

2. Check the seasoning and add herbs.

Variation: May be served as it is, or for a smoother soup liquidize or sieve it first.

Note: Make more than you need of this soup and you can use the leftover portion to get a special meal off to a delicious start. Liquidize the soup, then whip it up with some sour cream, a squeeze of lemon juice and just a little curry powder. Put it back in the fridge to get nicely chilled, then sprinkle with chopped fresh chives and serve.

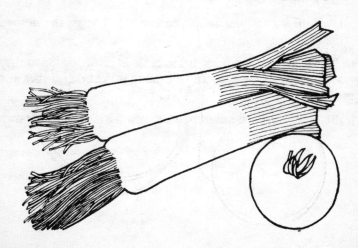

MIXED BEAN SOUP

Imperial (Metric)
4 oz (115g) mixed beans*
Bouquet garni
1 chopped onion
4 oz (115g) chopped swede or
 turnip
1 tablespoonful vegetable oil
¼ pint (140ml) vegetable stock or
 water
1 teaspoonful yeast extract
1 small tin baked beans
Seasoning to taste

American
½ cupful mixed beans*
Bouquet garni
1 chopped onion
¾ cupful chopped rutabaga or turnip
1 tablespoonful vegetable oil
⅔ cupful vegetable stock or water
1 teaspoonful yeast extract
1 small can baked beans
Seasoning to taste

1. Soak the beans overnight, then cook in remaining water and stock, or water with bouquet garni, until tender. You may need to add extra water during cooking.

2. Cook the onion and swede (rutabaga) or turnip in the oil for a few minutes, then add the stock or water and the yeast extract, and simmer until the vegetables are just cooked.

3. Add the tin of baked beans and combine with the rest of the soup. Check the seasoning.

4. If you like a thinner soup you can dilute it to the desired consistency.

Note: Whenever you are using beans cook an extra portion as they keep well in the fridge and can be used to make other dishes at a moment's notice.

* Health food stores sell mixed beans or you can combine your own favourites.

CREAM OF CARROT SOUP

Imperial (Metric)	American
1 small onion	1 small onion
1 stick of celery	1 stalk of celery
2 medium carrots	2 medium carrots
1 tablespoonful vegetable oil	1 tablespoonful vegetable oil
1 pint (570ml) milk or water	2½ cupsful milk or water
Seasoning to taste	Seasoning to taste
Good pinch of mixed herbs	Good pinch of mixed herbs
Approx. 2 tablespoonsful tahini	Approx. 2 tablespoonsful tahini
Chives to garnish	Chives to garnish

1. Finely chop the peeled onion and the celery. Peel and slice the carrots. Heat the oil in a large pan, add the onion and celery and sauté for 3 to 4 minutes. Add the carrots and continue cooking a few minutes more, stirring frequently.

2. Pour in the milk or water, season to taste and add the herbs. Bring to the boil, cover the pan and simmer over a low heat for about 20 minutes until the carrots are tender.

3. Transfer the soup to a liquidizer and blend it to a purée. Return it to the heat and warm through gently, then stir in enough tahini to give the soup a creamy texture.

4. Garnish with fresh chopped chives and serve immediately.

ONION SOUP WITH TOFU

Imperial (Metric)	American
3 medium onions	3 medium onions
½ oz (15g) polyunsaturated margarine	1 tablespoonful polyunsaturated margarine
1 pint (570ml) vegetable stock or water	2½ cupsful vegetable stock or water
Good pinch of sage	Good pinch of sage
½ tablespoonful wholemeal flour	½ tablespoonful wholewheat flour
Seasoning to taste	Seasoning to taste
Miso or soya sauce	Miso or soy sauce
5 oz (140g) tofu	5 ounces tofu
Parsley for garnish	Parsley for garnish

1. Peel and slice the onions. Melt the margarine in a saucepan, add the prepared onions, and sauté them for a few minutes until they begin to go transparent.

2. Add most of the vegetable stock and the sage, bring to the boil, then simmer for about 10 minutes, or until the onions are tender.

3. In a cup stir together the flour and remaining stock, add it to the saucepan, and continue cooking for 10 minutes more. Season, and add miso or soya sauce to taste (if using miso, blend it with a drop of water before adding to the pan).

4. Squeeze the tofu to remove the moisture, then crumble it so that it looks rather like cottage cheese. Add it to the saucepan and continue cooking gently for no more than 2 minutes.

5. Serve at once with parsley to add colour.

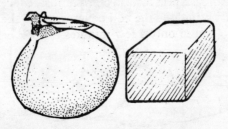

PEA SOUP

Imperial (Metric)	American
1 lb (455g) fresh peas	2²/₃ cupsful fresh peas
½ oz (15g) polyunsaturated margarine	1 tablespoonful polyunsaturated margarine
1 spring onion	1 scallion
1 pint (570ml) vegetable stock	2½ cupsful vegetable stock
½ tablespoonful chopped, fresh mint, or to taste	½ tablespoonful chopped, fresh mint, or to taste
Pinch of raw cane sugar	Pinch of raw cane sugar
Seasoning to taste	Seasoning to taste
2 tablespoonsful soured cream or yogurt (optional)	2 tablespoonsful soured cream or yogurt (optional)
Soya 'bacon' bits (optional)	Soy 'Bac-O-Bits' (optional)

1. Shell the peas and set aside. Melt the margarine in a saucepan, and gently sauté the chopped onion (scallion) for a few minutes.

2. Add the peas together with the stock, mint, sugar and seasoning, and bring to the boil. Simmer for about 30 minutes, or until the peas are tender.

3. When cool enough to handle, press the peas through a sieve or purée in a blender to make a thick smooth soup.

4. In summer serve it well chilled, with a spoonful of cream or yogurt swirled into each bowl. In winter serve it piping hot sprinkled with soya 'bacon' bits for a crunchy contrast — if necessary, the meat-eaters in your family can add chopped ham or bacon to their portion just before it is taken off the heat.

5. You can use frozen peas instead of fresh. Just reduce the amount of stock, and bring it to the boil before you add the peas. They will probably need only a few minutes to cook.

CREAMY SOYA SOUP WITH PEPPERS

Imperial (Metric)	American
4 oz (115g) cooked soya beans	1 cupful cooked soy beans
½ oz (15g) polyunsaturated margarine	1 tablespoonful polyunsaturated margarine
2 small green peppers	2 small green peppers
½ pint (285ml) vegetable stock	1⅓ cupsful vegetable stock
½ pint (285ml) milk	1⅓ cupsful milk
Seasoning to taste	Seasoning to taste
Croûtons to serve (opposite)	Croûtons to serve (opposite)

1. In a grinder, purée the well drained soya beans.

2. Melt the margarine in a large saucepan and add the peppers, cut into thin strips. Sauté them for 5 minutes, then add the stock and milk, bring to the boil, and simmer for 20-30 minutes, or until the peppers are soft.

3. Gradually stir in the soya bean purée, a spoonful at a time, making sure all the ingredients are well blended.

4. Season to taste and serve at once.

5. Golden brown croûtons (opposite) look attractive with this pale soup, but if you prefer, add a sprinkling of green herbs such as parsley or chives.

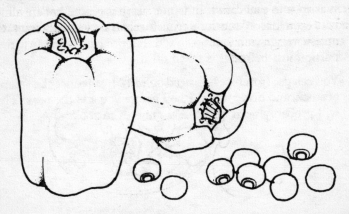

GOLDEN BROWN CROÛTONS

Imperial (Metric)	American
2 slices wholemeal bread	2 slices wholewheat bread
½ tablespoonful vegetable oil	½ tablespoonful vegetable oil
½ oz (15g) polyunsaturated margarine	1 tablespoonful polyunsaturated margarine

1. The bread is best if not too fresh. Cut it into very small cubes, then shallow fry them in a combination of the oil and margarine, stirring frequently, until they are crisp and evenly browned.

2. Drain and cool before using.

Note: You can make up more than you need, and keep them in an airtight tin for use at a later date.

Salads

The salad that does most for you is made up of a combination of green leaves, roots and fruits. Let the seasons be your guide and try whatever is cheap and plentiful in whatever combination sounds most appetizing to you. Just be sure to pick the freshest ingredients, use them as soon as you can, and do not cut them until you are almost ready to eat them — once the air gets to salads they lose their vitamin C content very quickly.

Green Leaves	Roots	Fruits
Lettuce	Carrots	Tomatoes
Watercress	Radishes	Cucumber
Mustard and cress	Onions	Peppers
Cabbage	Beetroots	Apples
Sprouts	Parsnip	Pears
Spinach	Celeriac	Grapes
Endive	Swedes (rutabaga)	Oranges
Chicory	Turnips	Grapefruit
Celery	Artichokes	Mushrooms
Leek		Dried fruit
Cauliflower		Avocado

With your salad you should have some form of protein, either as a hot savoury, or an an addition to your salad plate, i.e. seeds or nuts, ground or whole; cottage, cream or hard cheese; pulses such as cooked chick peas (garbanzo beans); lentils; peas or sweetcorn; eggs; cooked brown rice or other cereal; cold nut meat either left over from a previous meal, or from a tin. Many of the salad dressings given here will also boost your protein.

Suggested Salad Combinations

- Lettuce, celery, sliced banana.
- Celery, orange, cashew nuts, chopped chives.
- Avocado slices, apple, watercress, peanuts.
- Cauliflower, mustard and cress, sliced peach, wheatgerm.
- Cucumber, tomatoes, peas.
- Lettuce, melon chunks, orange slices, chopped nuts.
- Shredded cabbage and pineapple.
- Celery, green pepper, radishes, cottage cheese.
- Chopped apple, celery, walnuts.
- Lettuce, watercress, grapefruit, strawberries.
- Grated beetroot, peas and onions.
- Chinese cabbage, celery, tomatoes, Tahini Dressing (see page 44).
- Grated beetroot, apple, mustard and cress.
- Chopped apple and celery, grated parsnip.
- Shredded spinach, grated carrot and grapes.

- Grated cabbage, carrots, Cheddar cheese, nuts and raisins.
- Lettuce, chopped prune, grated apple, cress, almonds.
- Shredded red cabbage and red apples.
- Chopped green pepper, tomatoes, onion rings.
- Grated carrot and raisins.
- Grated cabbage, carrots, dried apricots.

To any of these salads you can add fresh or dried herbs for an extra taste treat.

Salad Dressings

CLASSIC DRESSING

1 part lemon juice or cider/wine vinegar
2 parts vegetable oil
Seasoning

1. Place all the ingredients in a screw-top jar with a well-fitting lid and shake well.

Variations:
- Add thin honey and English or French mustard to taste.
- Add crushed garlic and chopped parsley or mint.

YOGURT DRESSING

Imperial (Metric)
2 tablespoonsful plain yogurt
1 dessertspoonful vegetable oil
1 dessertspoonful lemon juice
1 dessertspoonful chopped herbs —
    parsley, mint, chives etc.
Seasoning

American
2 tablespoonsful plain yogurt
2 teaspoonsful vegetable oil
2 teaspoonsful lemon juice
2 teaspoonsful chopped herbs —
    parsley, mint, chives etc.
Seasoning

1. Shake all the ingredients together in a screw-top jar and keep refrigerated.

NUT DRESSING

Imperial (Metric)
1 heaped tablespoonful peanut (or
    other) butter
1 tablespoonful cider vinegar
1 dessertspoonful vegetable oil
A little water
Seasoning

American
1 heaped tablespoonful peanut (or
    other) butter
1 tablespoonful cider vinegar
2 teaspoonsful vegetable oil
A little water
Seasoning

1. Cream the first three ingredients together, add water to adjust consistency and season.

CREAM CHEESE DRESSING

Imperial (Metric)	American
2 oz (55g) cream cheese	¼ cupful cream cheese
½ teaspoonful French mustard	½ teaspoonful French mustard
1 tablespoonful vegetable oil	1 tablespoonful vegetable oil
1 tablespoonful cider or wine vinegar	1 tablespoonful cider or wine vinegar
1 tablespoonful milk	1 tablespoonful milk
Seasoning	Seasoning

1. Cream the cheese, mustard and oil, add the vinegar and milk. Season.

SALAD CREAM

1 part lemon juice or cider/wine vinegar
2 parts vegetable oil
3 parts evaporated milk
Seasoning

1. Shake all the ingredients well together in a screw-top jar.

Variations:
- Crumble 1 ounce (30g) blue cheese per tablespoonful of salad cream and mix it in with dressing.
- Add one teaspoonful of curry powder (or to taste).

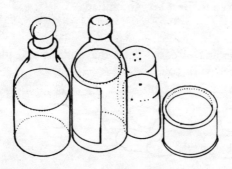

TAHINI DRESSING

1 part tahini
1 part warm water
Lemon juice
Paprika and seasoning

1. Mix the tahini and warm water to a smooth consistency and add
    lemon juice, a pinch of paprika and seasoning. Keep refrigerated.
    (Tahini is a paste made from crushed sesame seeds and is
    particularly high in protein, so when you add it to a salad you
    have a complete meal.)

CREAMY RUSSIAN DRESSING

Imperial (Metric)	American
¼ pint (140ml) mayonnaise	⅔ cupful mayonnaise
¼ pint (140ml) plain yogurt or soured cream	⅔ cupful plain yogurt or soured cream
Good handful chopped chives	Good handful chopped chives
Squeeze of lemon juice	Squeeze of lemon juice
Seasoning to taste	Seasoning to taste
Approx. 2 tablespoonsful tomato ketchup	Approx. 2 tablespoonsful tomato catsup

1. In a bowl combine all the ingredients, mixing thoroughly, and
    adding just enough tomato ketchup (catsup) to give the sauce
    a good colour. Best served chilled.

Variation:
A simple dressing of equal parts mayonnaise and plain yogurt is
especially good with coleslaw.

BLUE CHEESE WALNUT DRESSING

Imperial (Metric)	American
2 oz (55g) blue cheese	½ cupful blue cheese
½ oz (15g) walnuts	1 tablespoonful English walnuts
Seasoning to taste	Seasoning to taste
Approx. 2 tablespoonsful single cream or milk	Approx. 2 tablespoonsful light cream or milk

1. Soften the blue cheese by leaving it at room temperature for a while. Then put it into a bowl and mash well to make as smooth as possible.

2. Add the chopped walnuts and seasoning to taste.

3. Then stir in enough cream or milk to give it the consistency you want.

4. Serve at room temperature.

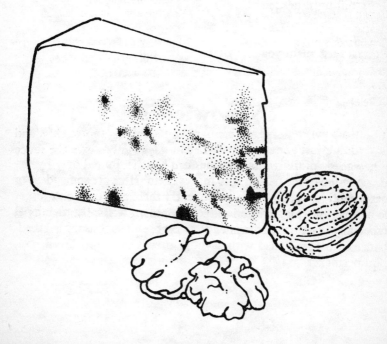

AVOCADO TOFU DRESSING

Imperial (Metric)	American
3 oz (85g) tofu	½ cupful tofu
1 tablespoonful lemon juice	1 tablespoonful lemon juice
1 tablespoonful vegetable oil	1 tablespoonful vegetable oil
1 small avocado, diced	1 small avocado, diced
Pinch of garlic salt	Pinch of garlic salt
Fresh, chopped dill (optional)	Fresh, chopped dill (optional)
1 spring onion, chopped	1 scallion, chopped
Seasoning to taste	Seasoning to taste

1. Drain the tofu well, cube, then put it into a blender with the lemon juice, vegetable oil, avocado, flavourings and seasoning. Combine thoroughly to make a smooth dressing.

2. Taste and adjust the seasoning if necessary. You can also add a drop more liquid (juice or oil) if you want a thinner consistency. Chill until needed.

Variation:
You can use plain yogurt instead of the tofu.

Sandwiches

The variety of fillings sandwiches can have is limited only by the imagination of the person who makes them! Here are some ideas to get you off to a good start — try one, try them all. And don't forget to be imaginative with the breads you use too. As well as the traditional wholemeal bread, experiment with sweet breads such as raisin bread, banana tea bread; also with savoury breads like corn bread, rye, pumpernickel.

COTTAGE, CREAM, CURD or RICOTTA CHEESE with:

- Tomato ketchup (catsup) or chutney
- Apple slices
- Apricot jam and almonds
- Chopped dates
- Thin onion and pepper rings
- Fresh or tinned pineapple
- Strawberry jam
- Banana slices
- Celery and a few caraway seeds

PEANUT BUTTER with:

- Curry powder and raisins
- Sliced banana
- Cream cheese and celery
- Crumbled milk chocolate
- Apple slices
- Honey and sesame seeds
- Thin slices of tofu
- Beansprouts
- Chopped black olives
- Jam or honey

EGGS:

- Scrambled, with chopped chives
- Boiled, mashed with grated cheese
- Boiled, mashed with mayonnaise and with green stuffed olives
- Boiled, mashed with grated courgette (zucchini) and parsley
- Scrambled, with beansprouts
- Scrambled, with pinch of curry powder

SALAD:

Use any crisp salad ingredients in whatever combination you fancy
— lettuce, cucumber, cress, celery, tomatoes, peppers, mushrooms,
beansprouts, finely chopped leeks or Brussels sprouts, raw cabbage,
carrots, etc.

Spread one piece of the bread lightly with yeast extract, tahini,
sesame spread or nut butter.

AVOCADO PEAR with:

- Nuts or seeds
- Boiled egg, chopped apple and mayonnaise
- Crunchy peanut butter
- Beansprouts
- Pineapple pieces
- Strips of red pepper
- Chinese cabbage, tomatoes, sesame seeds
- Cottage cheese with tiny piece of chopped garlic
- Chopped spring onion (scallion) and black olives

BANANA with:

- Honey and walnuts or roasted almonds
- Apricot jam
- Peanuts and raisins
- Chopped dates and coconut flakes
- Celery and apple slices
- Tahini
- Mashed with tofu and maple syrup
- Sprinkle of coarse raw cane sugar mixed with nutmeg
- Soya 'bacon' bits

AUBERGINE SPREAD

Imperial (Metric)
1 medium aubergine
1 crushed clove of garlic
1 finely chopped shallot
1 tablespoonful vegetable oil
Lemon juice
Seasoning to taste
Chopped parsley

American
1 medium eggplant
1 crushed clove of garlic
1 finely chopped shallot
1 tablespoonful vegetable oil
Lemon juice
Seasoning to taste
Chopped parsley

1. Bake the aubergine (eggplant) at 350°F/180°C (Gas Mark 4) for about 35 minutes (preferably when the oven is already being used). Allow it to cool, then split and scrape out the flesh. Chop the skin as finely as possible. Beat the flesh to cream it and add the skin.

2. Stir the garlic, shallot and oil into the aubergine (eggplant), making sure they are well mixed.

3. Finally, add some lemon juice, seasoning, and the finely chopped parsley.

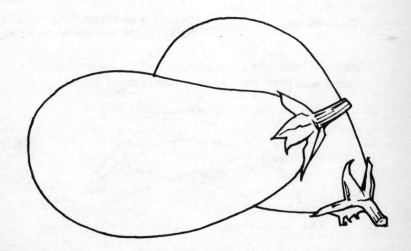

BEAN SPREAD

Imperial (Metric)	American
3 oz (85g) butter beans	⅓ cup Lima beans
1 small stick celery, finely chopped	1 small stalk celery, finely chopped
1 dessertspoonful vegetable oil	2 teaspoonsful vegetable oil
1 dessertspoonful tomato purée	2 teaspoonsful tomato paste
Seasoning to taste	Seasoning to taste

1. Soak the beans overnight, remove their skins, and cook in just enough water to cover them until tender. Drain the beans and then mash them.

2. Cook the celery in the oil and maybe a little water from the beans.

3. Add the tomato purée, mix in the bean purée and season.

Note: Keep both these spreads refrigerated and use as required.

SWEET BANANA SPREAD

Imperial (Metric)	American
1 large ripe banana	1 large ripe banana
1 tablespoonful tahini	1 tablespoonful tahini
Squeeze of lemon juice	Squeeze of lemon juice
Honey to taste	Honey to taste

1. Mash the banana in a bowl, and add all the other ingredients, mixing well until you have a smooth, creamy spread.

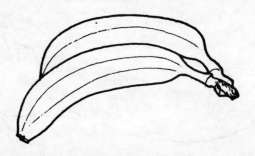

CURRIED TOFU SPREAD

Imperial (Metric)	American
3 oz (85g) tofu	½ cupful tofu
½ tablespoonful chopped onion	½ tablespoonful chopped onion
1 tablespoonful vegetable oil	1 tablespoonful vegetable oil
1 tablespoonful lemon juice	1 tablespoonful lemon juice
½ teaspoonful curry powder, or to taste	½ teaspoonful curry powder, or to taste

1. Drain the tofu well and then mash to make it as smooth as possible.

2. Blend in the onion, oil, lemon juice and curry powder, and adjust the taste by adding more lemon juice or curry powder if necessary.

Variations:

Omit the curry powder and substitute an equal quantity of chopped fresh herbs, blue cheese, diced avocado, chopped nuts or nut butter to flavour the tofu as liked.

ALMOND CHEESE SPREAD

Imperial (Metric)	American
2 oz (55g) cream cheese	¼ cupful cream cheese
1 oz (30g) chopped roasted almonds	¼ cupful chopped roasted almonds
1 tablespoonful mayonnaise	1 tablespoonful mayonnaise
Pinch of paprika	Pinch of paprika
½ teaspoonful horse-radish, or to taste	½ teaspoonful horse-radish, or to taste
1 tablespoonful chopped watercress	1 tablespoonful chopped watercress

1. Mash the cream cheese until smooth and creamy. Stir in the rest of the ingredients making sure they are well blended.

2. Taste and adjust the flavour to suit yourself. Chill briefly before using. This is particularly tasty with toast.

Note: All these spreads will keep for a few days, if not longer, providing they are refrigerated, preferably in a screw-top jar.

4.
QUICK AND EASY MAIN MEALS

Ideally cooking should be a leisurely pastime but, in today's busy world, it rarely is — and when you are cooking in a hurry, you are forced to use convenience foods. Don't feel bad about it. As a vegetarian you really do have a choice of the best. Many of the tinned foods you buy at health food shops have the minimum of additives and the maximum natural goodness. They are often very tasty, too, and you can always add some fresh vegetables or a salad to make up for what tinned food may lack in vitimins.

Cooking everything in one pot saves space, money, and washing up! So instead of putting your protein in one saucepan and your vegetables in another, throw them in together. Add vegetables to your omelette rather than serving them with it. Cook potatoes in with your bean stew, dumplings with your soup.

Invest in a wide-necked thermos flask and you can prepare and combine the ingredients in the morning, leave them to cook gently through the day — and come home to a ready-to-eat meal. Cheap to buy and costing nothing at all to run, thermos cookery offers one of today's best bargains for anyone who is short of time or space as well as money — it also helps when there are too many cooks in the kitchen!

Don't forget the advantages of cooking in advance. Pancakes can be frozen with foil between them ready to be unpeeled, stuffed and heated when required. Pasta dishes can be treated likewise. Grains and rice also keep well once cooked. Cheese can be grated and nuts ground in large amounts so they are ready for instant use. With a little forethought, you will find a rushed meal never need be an inferior meal.

PANCAKES

Imperial (Metric)	American
1/4 pint (140ml) milk	2/3 cupful milk
3 oz (85g) wholemeal flour	3/4 cupful wholewheat flour
Seasoning to taste	Seasoning to taste
1 egg	1 egg
Vegetable oil	Vegetable oil

1. Mix the milk with the flour to make a smooth paste. Add the seasoning.

2. Beat the egg and add it with enough milk to make a smooth pouring batter. Set aside for several hours.

3. Stir the batter well again before frying thin pancakes in oil.

4. Place spoonsful of filling on the pancakes, roll up, place in ovenproof dish and top with the sauce of your choice. You can also sprinkle your pancake with cheese and/or breadcrumbs and then dot with butter or margarine.

5. Heat for about 15 minutes at the top of a hot oven 425°F/220°C (Gas Mark 7).

Suggested fillings:

- Chopped spinach, onion, cream or grated cheese.
- Cottage cheese with chopped tomato and wholemeal breadcrumbs.
- Grated cheese, chopped celery and walnuts, wholemeal breadcrumbs seasoned and mixed with a little milk.
- Leftover vegetables combined with sauce or soup.
- Chopped leeks in a cheese sauce.
- Fried mushrooms and chopped walnuts (English walnuts).

PEASE PUDDING

Basic version:

Imperial (Metric)	American
1 lb (455g) split peas	2 cupsful split peas
1-2 oz (30-55g) butter or polyunsaturated margarine	2½ tablespoonsful - ¼ cupful butter or polyunsaturated margarine
Seasoning to taste	Seasoning to taste

1. Cover the peas with boiling water and leave to stand overnight, then simmer until tender — approx. 1 hour.

2. Drain the peas then mash them with a wooden spoon to a smooth, creamy consistency. Add butter and seasoning to taste.

Luxury version:

Imperial (Metric)	American
1 lb (455g) split peas	2 cupsful split peas
Seasoning to taste	Seasoning to taste
Bouquet garni	Bouquet garni
1 medium onion	1 medium onion
1-2 oz (30-55g) butter or polyunsaturated margarine	2½ tablespoonsful-¼ cupful butter or polyunsaturated margarine
2 small eggs	2 small eggs

1. Cover the peas with boiling water and leave to stand overnight.

2. Add more water, seasoning, herbs and onion and simmer until tender. Drain the peas and mash them with a wooden spoon.

3. Beat in the fat and the eggs. Season to taste.

4. Now place mixture in a greased basin, cover with foil, and steam for an hour.

Note: When the family is having pease pudding with boiled bacon, you can eat just the pudding with your vegetables, and still have a nourishing meal — especially if you make the luxury version.

Sauces

These mouth-watering and nutritious sauces can be served over vegetables, rice, grains, beans — whatever you fancy — to make an instant meal.

WHITE SAUCE

Imperial (Metric)	American
½ oz (15g) wholemeal flour	2 tablespoonsful wholewheat flour
½ oz (15g) butter, polyunsaturated margarine *or* 1 tablespoonful vegetable oil	1 tablespoonful butter, polyunsaturated margarine *or* vegetable oil
¼ pint (140ml) milk	⅔ cupful milk
Seasoning to taste	Seasoning to taste

1. Cook flour in the fat over gentle heat and stir until it bubbles.

2. Remove from heat and add the milk, stirring well to prevent lumps.

3. Simmer for a few minutes to thicken and cook. Season well.

Variations:
- Cheese — add up to 3 oz/85g (¾ cupful) grated cheese.
- Mushroom — add 4 oz/115g (1½ cupsful) sliced fried mushrooms.
- Onion — add a chopped onion, first cooked in the milk used to make the sauce.
- Herbs — add a single chopped herb, or a combination.

BROWN SAUCE

Imperial (Metric)
½ oz (15g) wholemeal flour
1 tablespoonful vegetable oil
1 teaspoonful yeast extract
¼ pint (140ml) vegetable stock or
  water
Seasoning to taste

American
2 tablespoonsful wholewheat flour
1 tablespoonful vegetable oil
1 teaspoonful yeast extract
⅔ cupful vegetable stock or water
Seasoning to taste

1. Cook the flour in the oil over gentle heat stirring occasionally, so that the flour darkens without burning.

2. Dissolve the yeast extract in the stock or water, then stir it into the fat and flour off the heat.

3. Continue cooking and stirring until sauce thickens. Season.

Variation:
Cook some finely chopped onion or celery and carrot in the fat before adding the flour. Serve sauce as it is, or liquidize first.

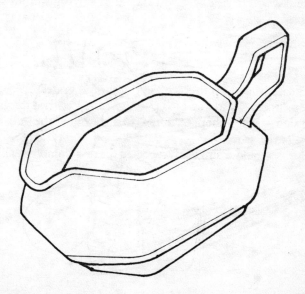

VEGETABLE SAUCE

Imperial (Metric)	American
1 onion	1 onion
2 sticks celery	2 stalks celery
4 medium mushrooms	4 medium mushrooms
2 medium tomatoes	2 medium tomatoes
Chopped parsley	Chopped parsley
Vegetable oil for frying	Vegetable oil for frying
1 oz (30g) chopped, blanched almonds	¼ cupful chopped, blanched almonds
Small carton cream — single, double or soured	Small carton cream — light, heavy or soured

1. Chop vegetables finely and fry in just a little oil until tender.

2. Remove from heat and stir in the almonds and cream.

Note: This sauce is delicious over vegetables, and can also be poured over the family's meat chops for a dish with a difference. If you have no fresh mushrooms or tomatoes to hand, use the tinned variety instead.

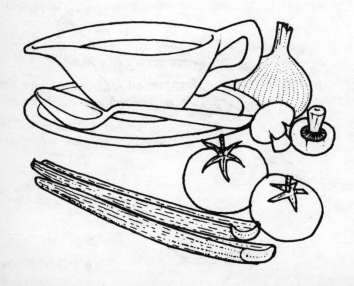

CURRY SAUCE

Imperial (Metric)	American
1 small onion, finely chopped	1 small onion, finely chopped
1 small apple, finely chopped	1 small apple, finely chopped
1 oz (30g) polyunsaturated margarine or butter	2½ tablespoonsful polyunsaturated margarine or butter
½ oz (15g) wholemeal flour	2 tablespoonsful wholewheat flour
1 teaspoonful curry powder (or to taste)	1 teaspoonful curry powder (or to taste)
1 teaspoonful curry paste (or to taste)	1 teaspoonful curry paste (or to taste)
½ pint (285ml) water with a little yeast extract dissolved in it	1⅓ cupsful water with a little yeast extract dissolved in it
Pinch of raw cane sugar	Pinch of raw cane sugar
1 teaspoonful desiccated coconut	1 teaspoonful desiccated coconut
1 teaspoonful chutney	1 teaspoonful chutney
1 teaspoonful sultanas	1 teaspoonful golden seedless raisins
Squeeze of lemon juice and seasoning	Squeeze of lemon juice and seasoning

1. Fry onion and apple in the melted margarine or butter until soft, then add the flour, curry powder and paste, and stir well.

2. After cooking gently for a few minutes stir in the water, bring to the boil, and cook until sauce starts to thicken.

3. Then add all ingredients remaining and simmer gently for 30 minutes to 1 hour. If food to be curried is raw, add it now and continue cooking for 30 minutes.

4. Serve on rice with such side dishes as chutney, nuts, cucumber in yogurt.

Note: Sauce can be kept in the fridge for a few days.

See Additions overleaf.

Additions:
- Add broken up cauliflower florets to sauce.
- Add a packet of frozen mixed vegetables.
- Add cubed aubergine (eggplant) and skinned courgettes (zucchini).
- Add cooked butter beans (Lima beans), lentils or chick peas (garbanzo beans).
- Add hydrated soya 'meat' chunks.
- Boil an egg, slice, lay on rice, cover with sauce.

GREEN ALMOND SAUCE

Imperial (Metric)	American
¼ pint (140ml) soured cream	⅔ cupful soured cream
1 tablespoonful chopped parsley	1 tablespoonful chopped parsley
1 spring onion	1 scallion
1 small green chilli pepper	1 small green chilli pepper
1½ oz (45g) roasted almonds	⅓ cupful roasted almonds
Seasoning to taste	Seasoning to taste

1. Put the soured cream into a blender with the parsley, onion, and de-seeded pepper, and blend until you have a smooth pale green sauce.

2. Chop the nuts coarsely and stir them into the other ingredients. Heat the sauce gently in a small saucepan, stirring frequently.

Note: Green Almond Sauce is the perfect topping for grain dishes, or vegetables — it also goes well with omelettes. As there is sufficient here for two or three servings, other members of your family might like to try it on fish (or keep the extra in the fridge for a day or two). The chilli pepper gives it a very strong flavour. If you prefer, use an ordinary green pepper for a more subtle taste.

Potato Dishes

POTATO CAKES

Mashed potatoes, either left over from a previous meal or cooked fresh, can be made into a variety of hot, tasty, and inexpensive dishes.

1. Mix them with chopped onion (cooked or raw), peas, any leftover vegetables, herbs, grated cheese and an egg. Make into small balls, flatten into cake shape, and shallow or deep fry for a few minutes.

2. Mix with sweetcorn, chopped onion and green pepper. Fry.

3. Make puff-balls with a gooey centre by enclosing small cubes of cheese in a ball of mashed potato, roll in beaten egg and deep fry.

JACKET POTATOES

If a meat dish is cooking in the oven, bake one or two jacket potatoes, add your favourite filling, and you will have as good a meal as the rest of the family. Scrub the potatoes, prick with a fork, and cook for about an hour. Then split open and fill with one of the following:

- Cream, cottage or grated hard cheese such as Cheddar, Edam, Gruyère
- Sweetcorn and butter.
- Baked beans and slices of fresh tomatoes.
- Scrambled egg and chopped chives.
- Spaghetti-type sauce made from soya 'minced meat'.

OMELETTE

2 eggs
1 tablespoonful water
Seasoning to taste
Knob of butter

1. Whisk the eggs, water and seasoning together lightly and then pour the mixture into a frying pan in which the butter has been melted.

2. Cook on medium heat until the omelette is set lightly on the bottom, then loosen it from the sides of the pan and tip the pan so that the liquid flows underneath.

3. When the eggs are set and the bottom is golden brown, add the filling, fold and serve.

Suggested Fillings: When these need to be cooked they should be kept warm until the omelette is ready.

- Lightly fried mushrooms.
- Lightly fried tomatoes with herbs.
- Mixed herbs, preferably fresh.
- 2 ounces (55g) finely grated cheese.
- A mixture of fried pepper, onion, mushrooms.
- Lightly fried onions.
- Drained sweetcorn.
- Spinach (mix with a little cream if liked).
- Asparagus tips.
- Fried or steamed leeks, chopped small.
- Beat some cottage cheese with the eggs before cooking for a really creamy omelette — do not cook too long.

SPAGHETTI

Imperial (Metric)	**American**
½ pint (285ml) water	1⅓ cupsful water
Pinch of sea salt	Pinch of sea salt
2 oz (55g) spaghetti	2 ounces of spaghetti
Knob of butter	Knob of butter

1. Bring the water and salt to the boil in a large saucepan.

2. Then hold the ends of the spaghetti in the boiling water until they soften, gradually turning the spaghetti so that it curls into the water. Continue until all the spaghetti is in the pan and then boil for about 10-12 minutes.

3. When just soft, drain and rinse in boiling water. Add butter to saucepan and stir drained spaghetti into the melted butter for one minute. Serve with Bolognese Sauce (page 64).

BOLOGNESE SAUCE

Imperial (Metric)
1 onion, finely chopped
1 carrot, finely chopped
2 oz (55g) mushrooms, finely
    chopped
½ clove garlic, crushed (optional)
1 oz (30g) butter or polyunsaturated
    margarine
4 oz (115g) soya 'minced meat',
    hydrated
Small tin tomatoes or 1
    tablespoonful tomato purée
1 oz (30g) Cheddar cheese

American
1 onion, finely chopped
1 carrot, finely chopped
¾ cupful mushrooms, finely chopped
½ clove garlic, crushed (optional)
2½ tablespoonsful butter or
    polyunsaturated margarine
1 cupful soy 'minced meat',
    hydrated
Small can tomatoes or 1
    tablespoonful tomato paste
¼ cupful Cheddar cheese

1. Lightly fry onion, carrot, mushrooms and garlic.

2. Add 'minced meat' and cook for a few more minutes. Blend in
   tomatoes or purée, adding a little water if necessary. Cover and
   simmer for 30 minutes.

3. Serve over spaghetti and top with grated cheese.

SWEETCORN FRITTERS

Imperial (Metric)
2 oz (55g) plain wholemeal flour
Seasoning to taste
¼ pint (140ml) milk
1 egg
10 oz (285g) tin sweetcorn or
    frozen equivalent
Vegetable oil for frying

American
½ cupful plain wholewheat flour
Seasoning to taste
⅔ cupful milk
1 egg
1½ cupsful canned sweetcorn or
    frozen equivalent
Vegetable oil for frying

1. Put the flour, seasoning, milk and egg into a bowl and beat until well blended.

2. Add sweetcorn (drain first) and mix evenly through the batter.

3. Gently fry spoonsful of the mixture in hot oil, turning once, for about 5 minutes or until fritters are a golden brown.

4. Sweetcorn fritters are not high in protein but there are a number of ways you can correct this. You can add a few teaspoonsful of powdered milk or soya flour to the mixture before cooking; cover the fritters with a protein-rich sauce; or serve a protein-rich dessert to balance your first course.

Note: This fritter recipe can be used to make a variety of different fritters. Instead of sweetcorn you can use lentils or split peas; cooked, drained and broken cauliflower; asparagus; fresh or tinned peas; cooked courgettes (zucchini), well drained and chopped up. Experiment with any leftovers you have around, too.

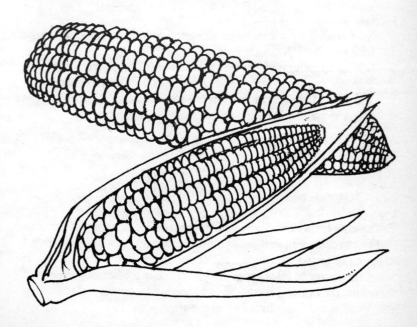

SPANISH LENTILS

Imperial (Metric)	American
4 oz (115g) lentils	½ cupful lentils
½ small tin tomatoes	½ small can tomatoes
1 small chopped onion	1 small chopped onion
1 chopped celery stick	1 chopped celery stalk
1 small chopped green pepper	1 small chopped green pepper
1 teaspoonful soya flour	1 teaspoonful soy flour
1 tablespoonful vegetable oil	1 tablespoonful vegetable oil
Bay leaf, nutmeg and sea salt	Bay leaf, nutmeg and sea salt

1. Wash the lentils thoroughly and put them in a saucepan with all the other ingredients.

2. Cover and cook gently until the lentils are soft and fluffy. (It may be necessary to add a little extra liquid during cooking.)

3. Serve hot with vegetables or rice, or cold with salad.

Variations:
- Stiffen mixture with wholemeal cereal or breadcrumbs and make into rissoles.
- Stir in some grated cheese and heat through in the oven.
- Put in a casserole and top with a mixture of grated cheese and wholemeal breadcrumbs. Brown under the grill.
- Use the basic mixture as a stuffing for vegetables.

Tinned Tasties

Eating out of tins need not be as drab as it sounds. Here are two quick-and-tasty meals you can make on those occasions when you forget to soak the beans overnight, but really fancy something filling. It is not necessary to stick religiously to these ingredients — nor even these kinds of beans. Just mix up whatever is available, add seasoning and some good fresh bread — and enjoy!

BAKED BEAN CASSEROLE

Imperial (Metric)	American
Small tin baked beans	Small can baked beans
3 tomatoes, sliced	3 tomatoes, sliced
1 small green pepper, finely chopped	1 small green pepper, finely chopped
1 small onion, finely chopped	1 small onion, finely chopped

1. Mix all the ingredients together, put in a covered saucepan and simmer gently for 30 minutes.

BUTTER BEAN HOT POT

Imperial (Metric)	American
2 tablespoonsful vegetable oil	2 tablespoonsful vegetable oil
1 small onion	1 small onion
1 small green pepper	1 small green pepper
1 stick celery	1 stalk celery
Small tin tomatoes	Small can tomatoes
Seasoning to taste	Seasoning to taste
Parsley	Parsley
Small tin butter beans	Small can Lima beans

1. Heat the oil and sauté the onion, pepper and celery, all finely chopped, until they begin to brown.

2. Add tomatoes and seasoning, plus parsley or any herbs you have to hand, cover pan and simmer sauce for 30 minutes.

3. Tip in drained beans and allow to heat through for 5-15 minutes (the longer you leave them, the more of the flavours they will absorb).

Vegetable and Nut or Seed Dishes

CABBAGE CRUNCH

Imperial (Metric)
2 oz (55g) pumpkin or sunflower
  seeds
Vegetable oil
1 small pepper
1 small onion
½ small green cabbage
Seasoning to taste
1 dessertspoonful soya sauce

American
4 tablespoonsful pumpkin or
  sunflower seeds
Vegetable oil
1 small pepper
1 small onion
½ small green cabbage
Seasoning to taste
2 teaspoonsful soy sauce

1. Toast seeds in a pan until they begin to pop, stirring constantly. Add oil, finely chopped pepper and onion, and cook briefly.

2. Shred cabbage and sauté with other vegetables for a further 5 minutes.

3. Season generously, dribble soya sauce over vegetables then cook for 10 minutes more, tossing frequently.

4. For extra crisp seeds, roast them separately and add them to the cooked cabbage just before serving. You can vary this dish by alternating with such vegetables as spinach or cauliflower.

SEEDED GREEN BEANS

Imperial (Metric)
4 oz (115g) green beans, fresh or
  frozen
2 oz (55g) sunflower seeds
½ oz (15g) polyunsaturated
  margarine or butter
Seasoning to taste

American
4 ounces green beans, fresh or
  frozen
4 tablespoonsful sunflower seeds
1 tablespoonful polyunsaturated
  margarine or butter
Seasoning to taste

1. Cook beans until just tender.

2. Fry the seeds in the melted margarine or butter until pale gold, then add the drained beans and cook gently until the beans start to brown. Serve at once.

3. For extra food value you can top with grated cheese and wholemeal breadcrumbs, and pop under the grill for a minute or two.

SPROUTS WITH CHESTNUTS

Imperial (Metric)	American
½ lb (225g) Brussels sprouts	8 ounces Brussels sprouts
6 oz (170g) chestnuts	6 ounces chestnuts
½ oz (15g) polyunsaturated margarine or butter	1 tablespoonful polyunsaturated margarine or butter
½ pint (285ml) vegetable stock	1⅓ cupsful vegetable stock
Freshly ground black pepper	Freshly ground black pepper

1. Wash and trim the sprouts and cook until tender.

2. Split the skins off the chestnuts and boil them steadily for 5-10 minutes. Remove the shells and inner skins while still warm. Put chestnuts in saucepan with half of the fat and the stock, cover and cook until soft.

3. Meanwhile, gently sauté the sprouts in the rest of the fat, shaking the pan frequently. Add the pepper.

4. Turn the chestnuts into the pan and mix them with the sprouts then eat while hot.

Note: Sprouts cooked this way can be served as a vegetable to the meat-eaters in your family too. They go well with most meats.

UNCOOKED NUT RISSOLES

Imperial (Metric)	American
1 tablespoonful grated nuts — any kind of combination	1 tablespoonful grated nuts — any kind of combination
1 tablespoonful crushed wholewheat breakfast cereal	1 tablespoonful crushed wholewheat breakfast cereal
1 teaspoonful yeast extract	1 teaspoonful yeast extract
1 teaspoonful tomato purée	1 teaspoonful tomato paste
½ green pepper, chopped finely	½ green pepper, chopped finely
1 stick celery, chopped finely	1 stalk celery, chopped finely
Seasoning to taste	Seasoning to taste

1. Combine the nuts and crushed cereal and then add all the other ingredients and mix well. If necessary, add a little extra water or stock.

2. Shape into rissoles and roll in chopped nuts, seeds or toasted crumbs.

Note: These quick and easy rissoles can be made with a variety of different raw or cooked vegetables but make sure they are chopped small. You can eat the rissoles with salad, hot vegetables, rice or grain dishes.

BEANSPROUT CASSEROLE
Serves 2

Imperial (Metric)	American
1 small onion	1 small onion
2 sticks celery	2 stalks celery
1 oz (30g) polyunsaturated margarine or butter	2½ tablespoonsful polyunsaturated margarine or butter
¼ pint (140ml) vegetable stock	⅔ cupsful vegetable stock
3 oz (85g) beansprouts	1½ cupsful beansprouts
2 oz (55g) cooked peas	⅓ cupful cooked peas
2 oz (55g) walnuts	4 tablespoonsful English walnuts
Soya sauce	Soy sauce
1 oz (30g) wholemeal breadcrumbs	½ cupful wholewheat breadcrumbs
Watercress or parsley to garnish	Watercress or parsley to garnish

1. Chop the onion and celery into small pieces. Melt the margarine in a frying pan (skillet) and sauté the onion and celery for 5 minutes, stirring frequently.

2. Add the vegetable stock and bring to the boil.

3. Transfer the mixture to a small ovenproof dish, together with the beansprouts, cooked peas and walnuts. Flavour with soya sauce and top with the breadcrumbs.

4. Bake at 350°F/180°C (Gas Mark 4) for about 20 minutes.

5. Garnish with the watercress or parsley and serve at once.

Note: This is sufficient for two average servings. You could have a good half of it, maybe with a grain dish or jacket potatoes, and the rest could be served as a vegetable to accompany a chicken or meat dish for the rest of the family.

SAVOURY 'MINCED MEAT'

Imperial (Metric)	American
1 teaspoonful yeast extract	1 teaspoonful yeast extract
⅓ pint (200ml) vegetable stock	¾ cupful vegetable stock
2 oz (55g) soya 'minced meat'	½ cupful soy 'minced meat'
1 chopped onion	1 chopped onion
1 grated carrot or equivalent of other vegetable (e.g. sliced mushrooms)	1 grated carrot or equivalent of other vegetable (e.g. sliced mushrooms)
2 tablespoonsful vegetable oil	2 tablespoonsful vegetable oil
1 tablespoonful tomato purée or ketchup	1 tablespoonful tomato paste or catsup
Herbs	Herbs
¼ oz (7g) wholemeal flour	1 tablespoonful wholewheat flour
Seasoning to taste	Seasoning to taste

1. Dissolve the yeast extract in the hot stock then hydrate the mince by soaking it in the liquid for 10 minutes.

2. Fry the onion and vegetables in the oil. Add the mince and remaining stock, the tomato purée and herbs, and after mixing thoroughly dredge with flour and simmer, stirring occasionally, until the sauce thickens.

3. Check that the vegetables are cooked, season, and serve as you would real minced meat.

Note: This versatile dish can also be topped with mashed potatoes and heated through in the oven to make a delicious Shepherd's Pie. Combine your 'minced meat' with tomato sauce and you have a bolognese sauce for your spaghetti. It can also be used in lasagne, moussaka, or to fill sausage rolls or pasties.

MUSHROOM AND PEPPER GOULASH
Serves 2

Imperial (Metric)	American
1 oz (30g) polyunsaturated margarine	2½ tablespoonsful polyunsaturated margarine
½ small onion	½ small onion
1 small pepper	1 small red pepper
½ lb (225g) mushrooms	4 cupsful mushrooms
2 teaspoonsful paprika, or to taste	2 teaspoonsful paprika, or to taste
Seasoning to taste	Seasoning to taste
2 tablespoonsful vegetable stock or water	2 tablespoonsful vegetable stock or water
¼ pint (140ml) plain yogurt or soured cream	⅔ cupsful plain yogurt or soured cream
2 teaspoonsful wholemeal flour	2 teaspoonsful wholewheat flour
1 hard-boiled egg (optional)	1 hard-boiled egg (optional)
Parsley to garnish	Parsley to garnish

1. Melt the margarine in a frying pan (skillet) and add the sliced onion and pepper. Sauté for 5 minutes, or until the vegetables begin to soften, then stir in the sliced mushrooms and cook for 5 minutes more.

2. Sprinkle in the paprika and stir well. Season lightly and add the stock.

3. Cover the pan and simmer the mixture for 10-15 minutes, or until the mushrooms are soft.

4. Mix together the yogurt and flour, and stir it into the other ingredients. Heat gently until warmed through.

Variation:
This goulash is delicious just as it is, but for extra protein you can sprinkle it with chopped hard-boiled egg, and for extra colour add some parsley.

COTTAGE CHEESE BURGERS

Imperial (Metric)	American
4 oz (115g) cottage cheese	½ cupful cottage cheese
Chopped chives	Chopped chives
Seasoning to taste	Seasoning to taste
1½ oz (45g) soya flour	⅓ cupful soy flour
1 large egg	1 large egg
1 oz (30g) wholemeal breadcrumbs	½ cupful wholewheat breadcrumbs
Vegetable oil for frying	Vegetable oil for frying

1. Mash or sieve the drained cottage cheese to make it smooth. Stir in the chives, seasoning, soya flour, and about half the beaten egg, mixing the ingredients well.

2. Use your hands to shape portions of the mixture into burgers — they will be fairly soft, but if they are too soft to handle, stir in a little more flour or some breadcrumbs.

3. Dip the burgers in the rest of the egg and then in the breadcrumbs making sure they are coated evenly.

4. Heat the oil and shallow-fry the burgers over a high heat, turning them once, until they are brown and crisp on the outside. Do not leave them cooking for too long. Drain on paper towels and eat at once.

Note: These burgers go well with green vegetables such as spinach; they also taste good with a tomato sauce.

5.

SHARING THE OVEN

As gas and electricity charges continue to climb, sharing the oven is more than just a convenient way of cooking; it makes sound economic sense. Luckily there are any number of vegetarian dishes that will happily share the oven with meat — slow cooking bean casseroles, quick loaves, hot-pots. One problem is that many of these dishes take less time than meat, so they have to be popped in later if you want everything to be cooked at the same time. The solution is to get the meat in the oven before you start preparing the vegetarian dish. That way you will have free surface space, and by the time it's ready to go into the oven, the timing should be about right.

You probably already bake your vegetables when you are having an oven-baked dish. But there may still be room to spare. Don't waste it — cook up some rice or beans, pasta or cakes for consumption on another day. Cooking well in advance is impossible for meat-eaters simply because meat is more inclined to 'go off', but the vegetarian who likes to save time and has the ability to get organized can do the bulk of a week's cooking in one go.

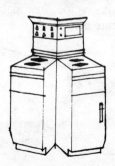

MOUSSAKA
Serves 4

Imperial (Metric)	American
½ lb (225g) soya 'minced meat'	2 cupsful soy 'minced meat'
1 small chopped onion	1 small chopped onion
2-3 tablespoonsful oil	2-3 tablespoonsful oil
1 tablespoonful tomato purée	1 tablespoonful tomato paste
1 tablespoonful water	1 tablespoonful water
Sea salt and cayenne pepper	Sea salt and cayenne pepper
2 medium aubergines	2 medium eggplants
4 oz (115g) grated cheese	1 cupful grated cheese
White Sauce (see page 56)	White Sauce (see page 56)

1. Fry the soya 'minced meat' and onion in a little oil until brown. Stir in the tomato purée and water. Season to taste and then cover and simmer for about 30 minutes.

2. Meanwhile peel, thinly slice and fry aubergines (eggplants) in the minimum of oil. Drain, then put a layer of aubergines in an ovenproof dish and cover lightly with cheese.

3. When 'meat' mixture is ready, pile it onto the vegetables topping it with a further layer of aubergine and cheese. Make the White Sauce and pour over the prepared dish.

4. Sprinkle with more grated cheese and bake at 375°F/190°C (Gas Mark 5) for 30 minutes. The top should be golden and bubbly.

Note: If the rest of the family prefer their moussaka to contain real meat, you can still use this recipe. Just make up separate portions, and cook them in separate dishes.

BUTTER BEAN LOAF

Imperial (Metric)	American
4 oz (115g) butter beans	½ cupful Lima beans
1 teaspoonful yeast extract	1 teaspoonful yeast extract
1 tablespoonful tomato purée	1 tablespoonful tomato paste
1 egg	1 egg
Chopped parsley or other herbs	Chopped parsley or other herbs
Crushed wholemeal breakfast cereal or breadcrumbs	Crushed wholewheat breakfast cereal or breadcrumbs
Seasoning to taste	Seasoning to taste

1. Soak the butter (Lima) beans overnight and simmer until soft. (It's a good idea to soak double the required portion and use the rest another day.)

2. Mash or liquidize the beans and add all the other ingredients, plus enough cereal or breadcrumbs to give the mixture a firm texture.

3. Bake in a greased dish for about 25 minutes at 350°F/180°C (Gas Mark 4).

Note: This loaf tastes delicious served hot with vegetables, and maybe your favourite sauce. If this portion is too much for your appetite, serve the leftover loaf with a salad later in the week.

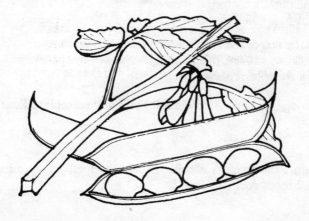

SAVOURY FLAN

Pastry Case:

Imperial (Metric)	American
4 oz (115g) wholemeal flour	1 cupful wholewheat flour
2 oz (55g) polyunsaturated margarine	¼ cupful polyunsaturated margarine
Water to mix	Water to mix

1. Use your fingers to mix the flour and margarine together to the consistency of fine breadcrumbs.

2. Add drops of water to the mixture until it can be formed into a ball.

3. Set aside for at least 30 minutes, then roll or press out and use pastry to line a tin or other suitable shallow dish. Bake blind for a few minutes to dry.

4. Then add prepared filling and bake for 30 minutes at 350°F/180°C (Gas Mark 4).

5. Serve hot or cold.

Filling:

Imperial (Metric)	American
1 beaten egg	1 beaten egg
¼ pint (140ml) milk or cream	⅔ cupful milk or cream
3 oz (85g) grated cheese	¾ cupful grated cheese
Chopped parsley or other herbs	Chopped parsley or other herbs
Seasoning to taste	Seasoning to taste

1. Mix egg and milk, add cheese, herbs and seasoning. Pour into case.

Variations:
● Reduce the quantity of milk and add chopped onion, tomato or mushroom cooked in oil.

- Add sliced lightly fried courgettes (zucchini).
- Add a few tablespoonsful sweetcorn.
- Fill pastry case with mixture of cooked chopped spinach, grated cheese, egg and milk. Top with more grated cheese.

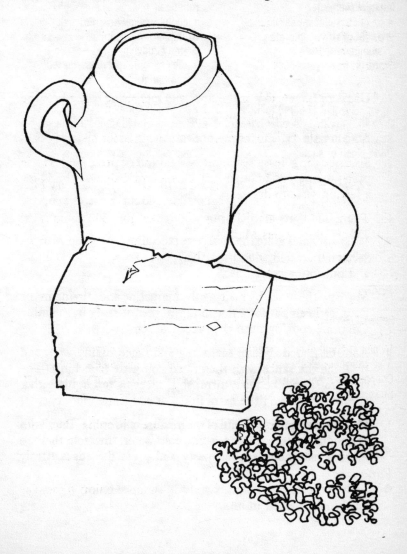

COURGETTE AND CHEESE PASTIES

Pastry as for Savoury Flan (page 78)

For filling:

Imperial (Metric)	American
1 small courgette	1 small zucchini
½ oz (15g) polyunsaturated margarine	1 tablespoonful polyunsaturated margarine
½ oz (15g) wholemeal flour	2 tablespoonsful wholewheat flour
Approx. ¼ pint (140ml) milk	Approx. ⅔ cupful milk
2 oz (55g) grated Cheddar cheese	½ cupful grated Cheddar cheese
Seasoning to taste	Seasoning to taste
Good pinch of sage	Good pinch of sage

1. Make up the pastry as described in the recipe for Savoury Flan (page 78). Roll it out as thin as possible, and cut into circles approx. 4 in. (10cm) across. Set aside.

2. Wash, dry and grate the courgette (zucchini). Sprinkle with sea salt and leave for a short time, then press to remove excess liquid and put into a bowl.

3. Make up the sauce by melting the margarine and stirring in the flour, sautéeing it for a few minutes, then stirring in the milk. Continue cooking until the sauce thickens.

4. Add the grated cheese, seasoning and sage, mixing well, and combine the sauce with the grated courgette (zucchini). The mixture should be fairly firm, so if it seems too liquid either sprinkle it with a little extra flour, or add some more cheese.

5. Put one or two teaspoonsful of the mixture onto each of the circles of dough, moisten the edges with cold water, then fold them to make a half-moon shaped pasty and press the edges firmly

together. Place them on a lightly greased baking sheet.

6. Bake at 400°F/200°C (Gas Mark 6) for about 15 minutes, or until the pastry is cooked and nicely browned.

Note: These are best eaten whilst hot or warm, though they *can* be taken for a packed lunch and eaten with a salad. As the quantities given here will make a good number of pasties, persuade someone to share them with you — the effort involved makes it hardly worth making less of them.

Variation:
A quicker filling can be made by mixing the courgette (zucchini) with grated cheese, or with a softer cheese such as cream cheese or ricotta. A pinch of dry mustard adds interest, as do a few peanuts, chopped almonds or sunflower seeds. You can also stir in part of an egg to make the filling set more firm.

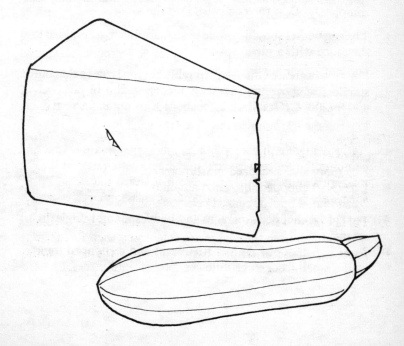

CHEESE SOUFFLÉ
Serves 2 or 3

Imperial (Metric)	American
½ oz (15g) polyunsaturated margarine	1 tablespoonful polyunsaturated margarine
½ oz (15g) plain wholemeal flour	2 tablespoonsful wholewheat flour
Seasoning to taste	Seasoning to taste
¼ pint (140ml) milk	⅔ cupful milk
3 oz (85g) grated cheese	¾ cupful grated cheese
2 eggs, separated	2 eggs, separated

1. Melt the margarine over a gentle heat, then remove from cooker and add the flour using a wooden spoon. Season with sea salt, freshly ground black pepper (plus a little cayenne and mustard powder for a tastier soufflé).

2. Add milk, bring to the boil and stir in the cheese until it has melted completely. Beat the egg yolks into the sauce.

3. The egg whites should now be beaten until stiff, and folded into the sauce with a metal spoon.

4. Pour into a greased dish — preferably not too large as the soufflé should rise above the edges when cooked. Put in hot oven at 400°F/200°C (Gas Mark 6) for about 30 minutes. Serve at once.

Variations:
Instead of cheese add to the basic sauce:
- 2 oz (55g) sliced, cooked mushrooms.
- 1 oz (30g) chopped, browned almonds.
- 2 oz (55g) chopped, cooked celery.
- 4 oz (115g) chopped asparagus and 1 tablespoonful single (light) cream.
- 2 oz (55g) chopped, lightly fried leeks and a chopped tomato.
- Half a small, cooked cauliflower, broken into pieces.

If others in your family prefer their soufflé to contain meat or fish, why not invest in some individual soufflé dishes or ramekins. Then you can use the same basic recipe, adding maybe cheese or nuts to your soufflé, and chicken, prawns, or whatever they want to theirs. Little soufflettes will probably cook quicker than a larger version, depending on your oven, so be careful the first time you make them.

Note: This is a very generous portion for one person, so if you choose one of the vegetable soufflés you have a complete and satisfying meal cooked in one dish. It can also be served as a starter.

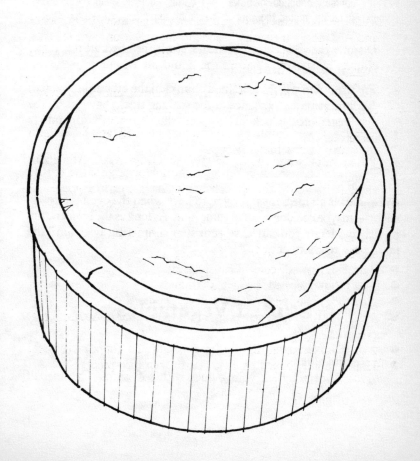

SOYA 'MEAT' STEW

Imperial (Metric)	American
1 teaspoonful yeast extract	1 teaspoonful yeast extract
1/3 pint (200ml) vegetable stock	3/4 cupful soy vegetable stock
2 oz (55g) soya 'meat' chunks	1/2 cupful soy 'meat' chunks
1 onion, coarsely chopped	1 onion, coarsely chopped
2 tablespoonsful vegetable oil	2 tablespoonsful vegetable oil
1 small tin tomatoes	1 small can tomatoes
Bay leaf and herbs	Bay leaf and herbs
1 stick celery, chopped	1 stalk celery, chopped
1 carrot, coarsely chopped, or other root vegetables, mixed together	1 carrot, coarsely chopped, or other root vegetables, mixed together

1. Dissolve the yeast extract in the hot stock, then hydrate the 'meat' chunks by soaking them in the liquid for 1 hour.

2. Fry the onion with the drained chunks in the oil until browned. Add the tomatoes, balance of the soaking stock, bay leaf, herbs and vegetables. Cook briefly and then turn mixture into a casserole.

3. Put in the oven and cook at 350°F/180°C (Gas Mark 4) for about 1 hour.

Note: This is an ideal meal for you to have when the oven is already alight — maybe cooking meat of some kind. As long as the temperature is fairly moderate you can leave your stew simmering away until the family are ready to eat.

Stuffed Vegetables

The Vegetables
Courgette (zuchini). Pick young ones with soft skins. Cut in half

lengthwise, use a spoon to scrape out pith and seeds, then steam or simmer until just tender. Drain, brush with oil, and pile stuffing on both halves. Cook at 350°F/180°C (Gas Mark 4) until stuffing is browned on top.

Green or red pepper. Cut closely round the stem and remove the pith and seeds. Blanch the peppers in boiling water for a few minutes, then drain and brush with oil. Fill with stuffing. Cook at 350°F/180°C (Gas Mark 4) until peppers are soft and stuffing is browned.

Tomatoes. Choose large, firm ones. Cut in half and scrape out pith and pips (add them to the stuffing mixture). Oil the skin, put in an ovenproof dish, fill with stuffing. Cook at 350°F/180°C (Gas Mark 4) until stuffing is browned.

The Stuffings
- Fried onion and wholemeal breadcrumbs bound with an egg — add a choice of ground nuts; grated cheese; fried mushrooms, peppers, sweetcorn.
- Cooked rice with fried onion, green pepper, celery, raisins.
- Cooked rice, chick peas (garbanzo beans), currants and peanuts.
- Any of the savoury mixtures given elsewhere in the book (e.g. Spanish Lentils (page 66), Nut Savoury (page 92), Butter Bean Loaf (page 77).

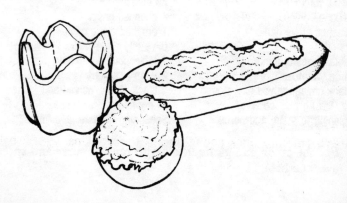

PIZZA

Base Mixture:

Imperial (Metric)	American
½ teaspoonful dried yeast	½ teaspoonful dried yeast
2 fl.oz. (60ml) warm water	¼ cupful warm water
½ teaspoonful sea salt	½ teaspoonful sea salt
4 oz (115g) wholemeal flour	1 cupful wholewheat flour
1 small egg	1 small egg
½ dessertspoonful vegetable oil	1 teaspoonful vegetable oil

1. Mix the yeast with the warm water and set aside.

2. Mix the salt into the flour in a warmed bowl. When the yeast mixture bubbles, add it to the flour with the beaten egg.

3. Knead to a soft dough and put it in a warm place to rise for 30 minutes. Then knead the dough again and pat out to an even thickness on an oiled baking sheet.

4. Brush with oil, leave to rise for a few more minutes, then add topping and bake for about 15 minutes at 400°F/200°C (Gas Mark 6).

Topping mixture:

Imperial (Metric)	American
1 chopped onion	1 chopped onion
1 crushed clove garlic	1 crushed clove garlic
Olive oil	Olive oil
2 tablespoonsful tomato purée	2 tablespoonsful tomato paste
2 large tomatoes	2 large tomatoes
3 black olives, halved and stoned	3 black olives, halved and stoned
3 oz (85g) grated cheese	¾ cupful grated cheese
Seasoning to taste, and herbs	Seasoning to taste, and herbs

1. Fry the onion and garlic in oil with tomato purée and spread over the base.

2. Cover with sliced tomatoes, olives and cheese. Season and sprinkle with some herbs and dribble a little olive oil over the top. (You can if you wish add or substitute chopped pepper, mushrooms or capers).

WHEAT GRAIN CASSEROLE

Imperial (Metric)
4 oz (115g) wheat grain
Vegetable oil
Water

American
½ cupful wheat grain
Vegetable oil
Water

1. Toast the grain in oil in a frying pan (skillet) until the grain begins to pop — move the pan constantly so the wheat does not burn.

2. Add water to cover wheat, bring to the boil, then simmer for about 45 minutes until tender. You may need to add more water during cooking. (As grain becomes sweeter the longer it is left, cook more than you need and keep the extra portion in the fridge).

3. Now transfer the grain to a casserole and top with one of the following mixtures. Cook covered in the oven for about 15-30 minutes until warm through. Use 325°F/170°C (Gas Mark 3).

Toppings:
● Leeks sautéed with chopped nuts and a touch of garlic.
● Cooked, broken-up cauliflower topped with a sprinkling of cheese.
● Spinach added to peanuts sautéed gently in oil.
● Frozen mixed vegetables topped with any of the sauces on pages 56 to 60.

RICE AND CHEESE LOAF
Serves 2

Imperial (Metric)	American
3 oz (85g) cooked brown rice	½ cupful cooked brown rice
4 oz (115g) grated cheese	1 cupful grated cheese
2 oz (55g) chopped nuts — walnuts are good	½ cupful chopped nuts — English walnuts are good
2 oz (55g) sunflower or sesame seeds	5 tablespoonsful sunflower or sesame seeds
1 large onion, finely chopped	1 large onion, finely chopped
1 large pepper, finely chopped	1 large pepper, finely chopped
2 eggs	2 eggs
Seasoning and herbs to taste	Seasoning and herbs to taste

1. Mix all ingredients together and put into a small, greased loaf tin. Top with more grated cheese.

2. Bake for 30 minutes at 350°F/180°C (Gas Mark 4). Serve hot or cold.

Note: Experiment with different vegetables and nuts when making this loaf. It is a simple recipe that adapts well, and tastes good whatever you put into it. Any leftovers can be eaten cold with salad.

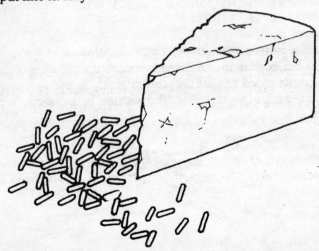

VEGETABLE CASSEROLE

Imperial (Metric)	American
6 oz (170g) potatoes	1 cupful potatoes
½ oz (15g) polyunsaturated margarine or butter	1 tablespoonful polyunsaturated margarine or butter
½ pint (285ml) water	1⅓ cupsful water
1 small onion, sliced	1 small onion, sliced
1 stick of celery, chopped	1 stalk of celery, chopped
1 leek, chopped	1 leek, chopped
1 carrot, chopped	1 carrot, chopped
2 tomatoes, peeled and sliced, or tinned equivalent	2 tomatoes, peeled and sliced, or canned equivalent
2 oz (55g) grated cheese	½ cupful grated cheese
Basil and mixed herbs	Basil and mixed herbs
Seasoning to taste	Seasoning to taste
1 small clove garlic, crushed (optional)	1 small clove garlic, crushed (optional)

1. Peel and cook potatoes for 10 minutes. Drain, and slice thickly.

2. Melt margarine in a pan, add water, bring to the boil and add onion, celery, leek and carrot. Simmer for 10 minutes, or until tender.

3. Drain vegetables, then layer them with the potatoes and tomatoes in a large ovenproof dish. Between layers add a sprinkling of the grated cheese, herbs, seasoning and garlic.

4. Finish with a layer of potatoes, then pour the stock from the cooked vegetables over the top, cover and cook at 375°F/190°C (Gas Mark 5) for about 1 hour. Top if liked, with fresh parsley; or a final sprinkling of cheese grilled briefly until brown and bubbly.

Note: You can, of course, use any combination of vegetables in this kind of casserole — the more, the tastier. Beans can also make a nice change.

MACARONI

Imperial (Metric)	American
2 oz (55g) wholemeal macaroni	1 cupful wholewheat macaroni
2 oz (55g) wholemeal breadcrumbs	1 cupful wholewheat breadcrumbs
A little hot milk	A little hot milk
1 egg, beaten	1 egg, beaten
1 small onion, chopped	1 small onion, chopped
1 small pepper or celery stick, chopped	1 small pepper or celery stalk, chopped
2 oz (55g) grated cheese	2 oz (55g) grated cheese
Pinch of sea salt and cayenne	Pinch of sea salt and cayenne
Mixed fresh or dried herbs	Mixed fresh or dried herbs

1. Cook the macaroni in salted water for about 15 minutes until tender, and drain.

2. Meanwhile soak the breadcrumbs in the milk, add the egg, vegetables and cheese. Season generously and flavour with your favourite herbs.

3. Put the macaroni into a casserole or ovenproof dish, pour the sauce carefully over the top and bake at 325°F/170°C (Gas Mark 3) for about an hour. The sauce should set when the dish is ready.

Note: Macaroni can, of course, be cooked on the top of your cooker for speed. This recipe is ideal for when you want a more unusual dish — it is also a clever way to use up leftover macaroni if you cooked too much.

LEEK PIE

Imperial (Metric)	**American**
1 leek	1 leek
2 oz (55g) chopped mushrooms	¾ cupful chopped mushrooms
1 tablespoonful vegetable oil	1 tablespoonful vegetable oil
1 cooked potato	1 cooked potato
1 hard-boiled egg	1 hard-boiled egg
2 oz (55g) cooked peas or sweetcorn	⅓ cupful cooked peas or sweetcorn
1 oz (30g) butter or polyunsaturated margarine	2½ tablespoonsful butter or polyunsaturated margarine
¼ oz (7g) wholemeal flour	1 tablespoonful wholewheat flour
½ pint (285ml) milk	1⅓ cupsful milk
2 oz (55g) Cheddar cheese	½ cupful Cheddar cheese
Dried herbs	Dried herbs
Seasoning to taste	Seasoning to taste

1. Cook the leek, drain and chop into small pieces. Sauté the mushrooms in the oil.

2. Grease an ovenproof dish and put in half the potato, cut into slices. Add half the egg, sliced, then the leeks, the mushrooms, and a spoonful of the peas. Repeat layers.

3. Make a sauce with the fat, flour, milk, cheese and herbs. Season. Pour sauce over the casserole, sprinkle with the cheese and a touch of paprika.

4. Bake for 20-30 minutes at 350°F/180°C (Gas Mark 4). Serve with salad or hot vegetables.

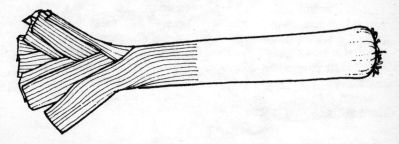

SOYA BEAN CASSEROLE

Imperial (Metric)	American
4 oz (115g) cooked soya beans	1/2 cupful cooked soybeans
2 oz (55g) grated cheese	1/2 cupful grated cheese
1 small tin tomatoes	1 small can tomatoes
1/4 pint (140ml) vegetable stock	2/3 cupful vegetable stock
1 tablespoonful vegetable oil	1 tablespoonful vegetable oil
Crushed bay leaf, parsley, thyme	Crushed bay leaf, parsley, thyme
2 tablespoonsful wheatgerm	2 1/2 tablespoonsful wheatgerm

1. In a greased casserole place alternate layers of beans, cheese and tomatoes until all ingredients have been used.

2. Mix the stock with the oil, bay leaf, parsley and thyme and pour over bean mixture. Sprinkle wheatgerm on top (plus a little more grated cheese if you like).

3. Bake the casserole, covered, at 350°F/180°C (Gas Mark 4) for about 30 minutes.

Note: This is a very hearty portion, so if you cannot manage it all, have it cold with a salad next day.

NUT SAVOURY

Imperial (Metric)	American
1 onion, chopped	1 onion, chopped
1 tablespoonful vegetable oil	1 tablespoonful vegetable oil
2 tomatoes, chopped and skinned	2 tomatoes, chopped and skinned
1 carrot, grated	1 carrot, grated
4 oz (115g) nuts, milled or chopped	3/4 cupful nuts, milled or chopped
2 oz (55g) wholemeal breakfast cereal or breadcrumbs	1 cupful wholewheat breakfast cereal or breadcrumbs
1/4 pint (140ml) vegetable stock *or* water with 1 teaspoonful yeast extract	2/3 cupful vegetable stock *or* water with 1 teaspoonful yeast extract
Herbs and seasoning to taste	Herbs and seasoning to taste

1. Fry the onion in the oil, add the tomatoes and carrot, and cook until soft.

2. Mix the nuts and cereal, and then add in all the other ingredients including the vegetable mixture.

3. Bake in a greased dish for 45 minutes at 375°F/190°C (Gas Mark 5).

Variation:

This vegetable dish can be served in a number of ways. Hot, it goes well with most vegetables; cold, it can be sliced and added to a salad. Shape the mixture into rissoles, dip them into egg and wholemeal breadcrumbs and you can fry your nut savoury. Add a beaten egg to the basic mixture and you have a lighter dish. And, for a complete change, replace the tomatoes with such vegetables as celery, mushrooms or chopped pepper.

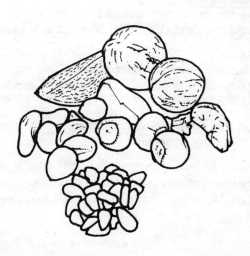

CAULIFLOWER OAT CRUMBLE
Serves 2

For topping:

Imperial (Metric)	American
1½ oz (40g) rolled oats	⅓ cupful rolled oats
1 oz (30g) grated Cheddar cheese	¼ cupful grated Cheddar cheese
1 oz (30g) polyunsaturated margarine	2½ tablespoonsful polyunsaturated margarine

For base:

Imperial (Metric)	American
½ medium cauliflower	½ medium cauliflower
2 oz (55g) grated Cheddar cheese	½ cupful grated Cheddar cheese
1 oz (30g) wheatgerm	¼ cupful wheatgerm
Good pinch of nutmeg	Good pinch of nutmeg
Seasoning to taste	Seasoning to taste

1. Put the rolled oats into a bowl with the grated cheese. Then use your fingertips to rub in the margarine to make a very coarse crumble.

2. Break the cauliflower into florets and steam or boil in the minimum amount of water for 10 minutes, or until tender. Drain well.

3. Mash the cauliflower to make a soft, smooth mixture — if it seems very dry, add a spoonful or two of the water in which it was cooked.

4. Stir in the grated cheese and wheatgerm and then add nutmeg and seasoning to taste.

5. Transfer the mixture to a small, lightly greased ovenproof dish. Spread the prepared crumble over the top, pressing it down lightly. Bake at 375°F/190°C (Gas Mark 5) for 20 minutes, or

until the topping is lightly browned.

6. Serve at once. This is enough for two portions — another member
    of your family might like to share it with you, adding a slice or
    two of cold meat.

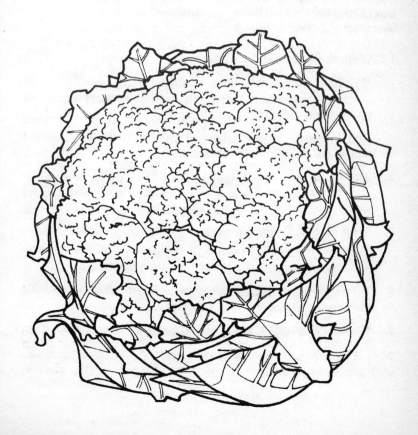

BULGUR BAKE

Imperial (Metric)	American
4 oz (115g) bulgur	½ cupful bulgur
½ oz (15g) polyunsaturated margarine	1 tablespoonful polyunsaturated margarine
1 small onion	1 small onion
1 small pepper	1 small pepper
½ pint (285ml) vegetable stock or water	1⅓ cupsful vegetable stock or water
Seasoning to taste	Seasoning to taste
1 egg	1 egg
2½ fl.oz. (75ml) plain yogurt	Approx. ¼ cupful plain yogurt
1 oz (30g) grated Cheddar cheese	¼ cupful grated Cheddar cheese
Good pinch of paprika	Good pinch of paprika

1. Wash the bulgur and set aside.

2. Melt half of the margarine in a pan and gently sauté the sliced onion and pepper until they begin to soften. Remove them from the pan and place them on one side.

3. Add the rest of the margarine and when it has melted, sauté the bulgur for a few minutes to brown it.

4. Add the stock and seasoning to taste, bring to the boil, cover, and simmer for 15 minutes by which time most of the liquid should have been absorbed. Remove the pan from the heat and drain off any excess liquid.

5. Add the onion and pepper to the bulgur, then the beaten egg and enough yogurt to make the mixture creamy.

6. Turn the mixture into a small greased ovenproof dish and sprinkle with the grated cheese and paprika.

7. Bake at 350°F/180°C (Gas Mark 4) for 20-30 minutes, or until set.

Note: Any leftovers can be used to thicken soups or to stuff vegetables such as marrow (squash) rings or peppers. Or try mixing the leftovers with more cheese and part of a beaten egg, and making them into rissoles to shallow-fry. Other grains can be cooked in the same way, millet being especially suitable.

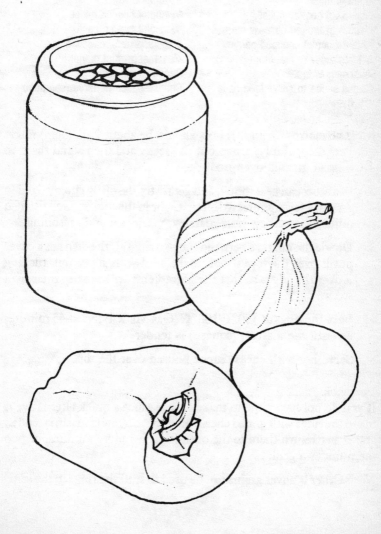

MARROW RINGS WITH MILLET STUFFING

Imperial (Metric)	American
2 marrow rings	2 squash rings
1 tablespoonful vegetable oil	1 tablespoonful vegetable oil
½ small onion	½ small onion
2 oz (55g) cooked millet	⅓ cupful cooked millet
2 oz (55g) broken cashew nuts	½ cupful broken cashew nuts
1 tablespoonful chopped parsley	1 tablespoonful chopped parsley
½-1 teaspoonful marjoram	½-1 teaspoonful marjoram
Seasoning to taste	Seasoning to taste
Cheese sauce to serve (see page 56)	Cheese sauce to serve (see page 56)

1. The marrow (squash) slices should be about 2 in. (5cm) thick. Peel them thinly, scoop out the seeds and then stand them in a small greased ovenproof dish.

2. In a saucepan heat the oil, and gently fry the finely chopped onion for just a few minutes to soften it. Stir in the cooked, well-drained millet, the cashew nuts, parsley, marjoram and seasoning.

3. Divide the mixture between the two rings. If the dish has a cover put it over the top; if not, make a lid with silver foil, tucking it over the edges so that the ingredients will cook in their own steam.

4. Bake the rings at 350°F/180°C (Gas Mark 4) for 30-45 minutes or until the marrow (squash) is tender.

5. Serve hot with cheese sauce poured over the top.

Variation:
If you do not have time to make cheese sauce a quick alternative is to top the rings with grated cheese once the marrow (squash) is tender, and either return them to the oven for a few more minutes, or pop them under a grill.

Note: Other leftover grains can be used to stuff the rings in the same way, adding a few nuts, cooked beans or lentils, and whatever herbs you have handy. Beaten egg, grated cheese or a spoonful of tahini can be stirred in to add protein and give a softer consistency.

LASAGNE

Imperial (Metric)	American
2 oz (55g) wholemeal lasagne	2 ounces wholewheat lasagne
4 oz (115g) cottage or curd cheese	½ cupful cottage or curd cheese
1 small egg	1 small egg
½ small onion, fried	½ small onion, fried
2 teaspoonsful soft raw cane sugar	2 teaspoonsful soft raw cane sugar
1 small carton plain yogurt (you may need more)	1 small carton plain yogurt (you may need more)

1. Cook the lasagne in boiling salted water for about 15 minutes until tender. Drain and place in a bowl of cold water (this is so it stays pliable).

2. Mix the cheese, egg and onion together, plus one teaspoonful of sugar.

3. Stir the rest of the sugar into the yogurt and then put a good layer of this mixture into a small casserole. Top with a layer of lasagne, a few spoonsful of yogurt, another layer of lasagne, a few spoonsful of cheese. Continue in this way until all ingredients are used up, finishing with a thick layer of cheese.

4. Now cover the top completely with yogurt and a final sprinkling of sugar. Cook for about 30 minutes at 375°F/180°C (Gas Mark 4).

5. As an interesting change, try alternating spinach and cheese with the lasagne.

6.

VEGAN DISHES

AVOCADO RISOTTO
Serves 2

Imperial (Metric)	American
4 oz (115g) green beans	4 ounces green beans
1 tablespoonful vegetable oil	1 tablespoonful vegetable oil
1 small onion	1 small onion
4 oz (115g) brown rice	½ cupful brown rice
½ pint (285ml) vegetable stock	1⅓ cupsful vegetable stock
1 oz (30g) walnuts	2 tablespoonsful English walnuts
1 firm avocado	1 firm avocado
Seasoning to taste	Seasoning to taste

1. Trim the beans, slice them, and steam until cooked but still crisp.

2. Heat the oil in a saucepan, add the finely sliced onion, and sauté until transparent.

3. Stir in the rice and cook for a few minutes, then add the stock and bring to the boil.

4. Reduce the heat and simmer the rice for about 15-20 minutes, or until the liquid has been absorbed and the rice grains are cooked but still quite firm.

5. Stir in the drained beans and the chopped walnuts. Peel, stone and coarsely chop the avocado and mix it in with the other ingredients. Serve whilst still piping hot.

Variation:
If you prefer you can serve the risotto with the sliced avocado arranged
decoratively on top, in which case toss it in lemon juice first.

ADUKI BEAN RISSOLES

Imperial (Metric)	American
4 oz (115g) aduki beans	½ cupful aduki beans
Approx. 2 oz (55g) wholemeal breadcrumbs	Approx. 1 cupful wholewheat breadcrumbs
½ tablespoonful finely grated onion	½ tablespoonful finely grated onion
½ tablespoonful chopped parsley	½ tablespoonful chopped parsley
1 teaspoonful yeast extract	1 teaspoonful yeast extract
1 oz (30g) wheatgerm	¼ cupful wheatgerm
Vegetable oil for frying	Vegetable oil for frying

1. Cook the beans in plenty of water — they will cook quicker if
   soaked first. (This is another ideal way to use up leftovers). When
   soft, mash the beans to make a thick paste.

2. Combine this with the breadcrumbs to make a mixture firm
   enough to shape, but not too dry and then add the onion, parsley
   and yeast extract.

3. Divide into rissoles and coat each one evenly with wheatgerm.

4. Shallow fry in hot vegetable oil until heated through and eat at
   once. If some are left over they can be used another day.

Variation:
For Uncooked Aduki Bean Rissoles, follow the same method up to
the point where you shape them, but roll them in finely chopped
nuts instead of the wheatgerm, chill briefly, then serve with a salad.

CUCUMBER IN BÉCHAMEL SAUCE

Imperial (Metric)	American
½ pint (285ml) soya milk	1⅓ cupsful soy milk
¼ small onion	¼ small onion
½ carrot	½ carrot
½ stick celery	½ stalk celery
1 tablespoonful vegetable oil	1 tablespoonful vegetable oil
1 oz (30g) wholemeal flour	¼ cupful wholewheat flour
Seasoning to taste	Seasoning to taste
1 cucumber	1 cucumber
1 oz (30g) wholemeal breadcrumbs	½ cupful wholewheat breadcrumbs
Parsley	Parsley

1. Put the milk into a saucepan with the very finely chopped onion, carrot and celery, bring to the boil and remove from the heat.

2. Cover the pan and leave for 10-15 minutes for the flavours to be absorbed by the milk, then strain it and discard the vegetables.

3. Heat the oil in a clean saucepan and sprinkle in the flour, cooking it gently for a few minutes.

4. Stir in the milk and continue cooking and stirring until the sauce comes to the boil and thickens. Season to taste.

5. Dice the clean cucumber and lay it in the base of a small, lightly oiled dish. Top with a generous helping of the sauce, sprinkle with breadcrumbs, and bake at 400°F/200°C (Gas Mark 6) for 10 minutes.

6. Garnish with parsley. Delicious served with a grain dish and a tomato salad.

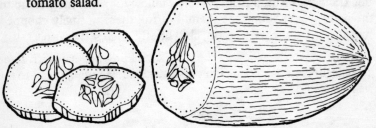

TAGLIATELLE WITH CARROT SAUCE

Imperial (Metric)	American
2 oz (55g) cooked green peas	⅓ cupful cooked green peas
1 large carrot	1 large carrot
½ small onion	½ small onion
1 tablespoonful vegetable oil	1 tablespoonful vegetable oil
½ oz (15g) wholemeal flour	2 tablespoonsful wholewheat flour
Approx. ⅓ pint (200ml) vegetable stock	Approx. ¾ cupful vegetable stock
1 tablespoonful chopped parsley	1 tablespoonful chopped parsley
Seasoning to taste	Seasoning to taste
3 oz (85g) wholemeal tagliatelle	3 ounces wholewheat tagliatelle

1. The green peas can be fresh or frozen, freshly cooked or leftovers. Drain them well and set aside. Peel and cut the carrot into cubes. Slice the onion.

2. Heat the oil and gently fry the carrot and onion for a few minutes, stirring frequently, then remove them from the pan and set aside.

3. Stir the flour into the remaining oil (you may need to add a drop more) and sauté for 1 minute. Stir in the vegetable stock.

4. Bring to the boil and cook for a few minutes, stirring frequently to keep the sauce smooth.

5. Add the parsley, seasoning, and the prepared vegetables, cover the pan, and cook gently for 10 minutes more, adding extra stock if necessary.

6. Meanwhile cook the tagliatelle in boiling salted water for 10 minutes, or until just tender. Drain and serve topped with the sauce.

Note: Although the peas and wholemeal pasta both contain protein, you can boost this — if you like — by sprinkling the dish with some flaked (slivered) almonds. They also make a delicious contrast to the vegetables and sauce.

MUSHROOM CABBAGE ROLLS

Imperial (Metric)	American
2 large Chinese cabbage leaves	2 large Chinese cabbage leaves
4 tablespoonsful cooked brown rice or bulgur	1/3 cupful cooked brown rice or bulgur
1 tablespoonful vegetable oil	1 tablespoonful vegetable oil
1 small onion	1 small onion
1/4 clove garlic, crushed (optional)	1/4 clove garlic, crushed (optional)
2 oz (55g) mushrooms	1 cupful mushrooms
2 oz (55g) sunflower seeds	1/2 cupful sunflower seeds
Seasoning to taste	Seasoning to taste

1. Trim the stalks off the cabbage leaves and then drop the leaves in boiling salted water and cook for 2 minutes. Drain well and leave to cool.

2. Put the rice or bulgur into a bowl. Heat the oil in a saucepan and gently sauté the sliced onion and crushed garlic until the onion begins to go transparent.

3. Stir in the sliced mushrooms and cook a few minutes more, stirring frequently, until all the vegetables are soft.

4. Tip this mixture into the bowl with the rice or bulgur, add the seeds and seasoning, and mix very well.

5. Place an equal amount of the filling near the base of the leaves, and roll them up carefully to form a parcel, turning the sides in so that the filling stays in place.

6. Put them side by side in a shallow ovenproof dish and bake, covered, at 350°F/180°C (Gas Mark 4) for about 30 minutes, or until heated right through. Serve at once.

7. A spicy tomato sauce goes well with these mushroom cabbage rolls.

Note: When a dish like this is made for just one person it is rarely worth cooking the grains specially for it — much better to cook a little extra a day or two before. If you only have a spoonful each of different grains available, try mixing them together for an unusual but just as tasty filling!

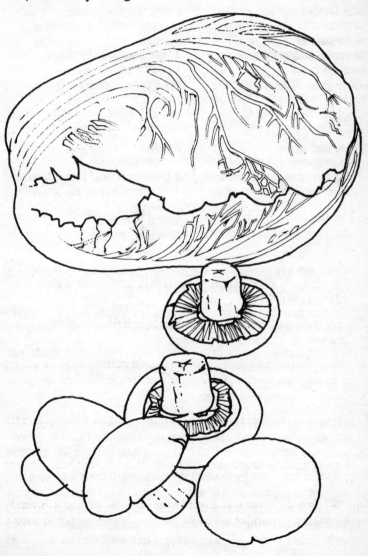

ONION CRUMBLE
Serves 2

For crumble:

Imperial (Metric)	American
4 oz (115g) wholemeal flour	1 cupful wholewheat flour
2 oz (55g) vegan margarine	¼ cupful vegan margarine
Good pinch of thyme	Good pinch of thyme

For base:

Imperial (Metric)	American
3 medium onions	3 medium onions
1-2 tablespoonsful peanut butter	1-2 tablespoonsful peanut butter
1 teaspoonful yeast extract, or to taste	1 teaspoonful yeast extract, or to taste
Thyme to taste	Thyme to taste
Seasoning to taste	Seasoning to taste

1. Make the crumble first. Put the flour in a bowl and then use your fingertips to rub in the margarine to make a crumb-like mixture. Stir in the thyme.

2. Peel and slice the onions and steam or boil them in the minimum amount of water for 10 minutes.

3. Drain them lightly then stir in the peanut butter and yeast extract, blending them well so that they dissolve to make a creamy sauce. Add the thyme and seasoning.

4. Spoon the mixture into a small ovenproof dish and sprinkle the top with the crumble, pressing it down gently to make an even topping. Bake at 375°F/190°C (Gas Mark 5) for 20 minutes.

Note: As it is not very good cold, it is not worth cooking more than you will eat. So if no-one will share it with you, make up the same amounts of the crumble and the filling, then keep the crumble in a cellophane bag in the freezer, ready for instant use another time. The onion mixture can be eaten another day with vegetables, on top of rice or another grain, or as a filling for pancakes (crêpes) or a flan.

If you have no vegan margarine available for the crumble, use oil instead, adding just enough to get a crumb-like consistency. The results will be different, but just as edible!

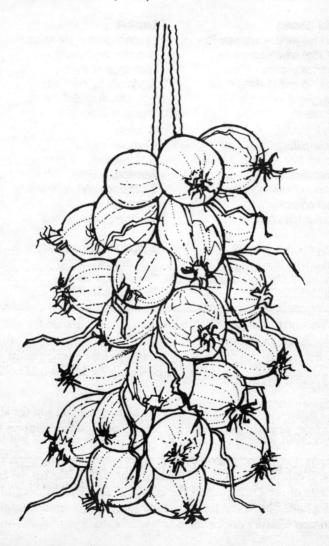

PANCAKES PEPERONATA
Serves 2

For the pancakes:

Imperial (Metric)	American
2 oz (55g) plain wholemeal flour	½ cupful plain wholewheat flour
1 oz (30g) soya flour	¼ cupful soy flour
Pinch of sea salt	Pinch of sea salt
Approx. ¼ pint (140ml) water	Approx. ⅔ cupful water
1 teaspoonful vegetable oil	1 teaspoonful vegetable oil
Vegetable oil for frying	Vegetable oil for frying

For the filling:

Imperial (Metric)	American
2 tablespoonsful vegetable oil	2 tablespoonsful vegetable oil
1 small onion	1 small onion
½ clove garlic, crushed	½ clove garlic, crushed
1 bay leaf	1 bay leaf
2 medium green peppers	2 medium green peppers
2 small tomatoes	2 small tomatoes
Seasoning to taste	Seasoning to taste
3 oz (85g) tofu	½ cupful tofu

1. To make the pancake (crêpe) batter, mix the flours and salt together in a bowl, then gradually add the water, stirring continuously to remove any lumps. Whisk energetically, beat in the oil, cover, and leave in a cool place for at least half an hour, preferably longer.

2. To make the peperonata, heat the oil in a pan and add the sliced onion, crushed garlic and bay leaf. Cook for a few minutes then stir in the sliced peppers and cook a little longer.

3. Add the tomatoes, skinned and chopped, and seasoning and cover the pan. Cook over a low heat for about 30 minutes, or until the mixture is thick and dry.

4. Drain the tofu, mash coarsely with a fork, then stir it into the peperonata mixture, making sure it is distributed evenly. Leave on the heat for just a few minutes more.

5. Before making the pancakes, whisk the batter again, and if necessary add a little water so that it pours easily.

6. Heat a drop of oil in a frying pan (skillet) and, when it begins to smoke, pour in a thin layer of the batter. Cook gently until the pancake is lightly browned underneath, giving the pan an occasional shake to prevent sticking. Flip pancake and cook the other side, then set aside in a warm place. Use up the rest of the batter in the same way.

7. When ready to eat, divide the peperonata between the pancakes, fold, and serve immediately.

Note: Extra pancakes can be kept in an airtight container to use another day or keep the batter mixture in the fridge and make them fresh when needed — pancakes also freeze well. Any extra filling can be used in a different recipe, made into a soup, or simply poured over the top of the pancakes.

Variations:
Pancakes made in this way can be filled with a variety of different mixture. Try soya meat bolognaise; lentils in tomato sauce; vegetables and nuts, especially good if mixed into a béchamel sauce (see Cucumber in Béchamel Sauce, page 102 for the vegan version).

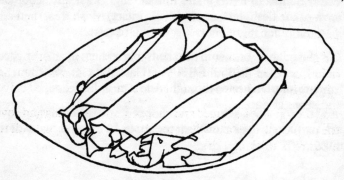

SPICED AUBERGINE WITH CHICK PEAS

Serves 1 or 2

Imperial (Metric)	American
1 medium aubergine	1 medium eggplant
2 tablespoonsful vegetable oil	2 tablespoonsful vegetable oil
½ small onion	½ small onion
½ green pepper	½ green pepper
Good pinch of cumin	Good pinch of cumin
Good pinch of ginger	Good pinch of ginger
Good pinch of coriander	Good pinch of coriander
2 oz (55g) cooked chick peas	¼ cupful cooked garbanzo beans
Seasoning to taste	Seasoning to taste
Chives to garnish	Chives to garnish

1. Put the washed aubergine (eggplant) in a shallow pan and bake at 400°F/200°C (Gas Mark 6) for 40-50 minutes, or until soft. (If you want to take advantage of the oven being on to cook another dish, this can be prepared a day before you intend to eat it). Leave to cool slightly.

2. Heat the oil in a frying pan (skillet) and gently fry the very finely chopped onion and pepper for a few minutes, then stir in the spices and continue cooking until the onion is soft.

3. Grind the well drained chick peas (garbanzos), and add them to the onion and spices, mixing well.

4. Cut the aubergine (eggplant) in half lengthways and scoop out most of the flesh, leaving the shells intact. Mash this, then add it to the other ingredients, seasoning to taste.

5. Pile the mixture back into the shells, place them in an ovenproof dish, and bake at 350°F/180°C (Gas Mark 4) for about 20 minutes, or until heated through. Add a garnish of chopped chives and serve at once.

Note: This quantity makes one very generous helping, or two average helpings.

LENTIL AND WALNUT LOAF
Serves 4

Imperial (Metric)
1 tablespoonful vegetable oil
1 large onion
6 oz (170g) red split lentils
¾ pint (425ml) water *or* vegetable
  stock
1 teaspoonful yeast extract
1 tablespoonful crushed rosemary,
  or to taste
Seasoning to taste
4 oz (115g) walnuts
Approx. 1 oz (30g) wholemeal
  breadcrumbs

American
1 tablespoonful vegetable oil
1 large onion
¾ cupful red split lentils
2 cupsful water *or* vegetable stock
1 teaspoonful yeast extract
1 tablespoonful crushed rosemary,
  or to taste
Seasoning to taste
¾ cupful English walnuts
Approx. ½ cupful wholewheat
  breadcrumbs

1. Heat the oil in a large pan, then sauté the sliced onion for 5 minutes. Add the lentils, stir and cook briefly. Pour on the water or stock and bring to the boil.

2. Stir in the yeast extract, add the herbs and seasoning, cover the pan and simmer all the ingredients until most of the liquid has been absorbed.

3. Chop or coarsely grind the walnuts and stir them into the lentil mixture. If it is still very moist, add some breadcrumbs until you have a thick but not too dry purée.

4. Turn into a lightly greased small loaf tin and bake at 400°F/200°C (Gas Mark 6) for 30-40 minutes.

Note: This quantity is enough for four average servings, but the loaf is hardly worth making if you use less. If no-one in your family wants to try it, you can always use any leftovers as a sandwich spread; made into rissoles; as a stuffing for vegetables; or to make 'sausage' rolls. If serving it to guests make it look more attractive by covering the top with slices of tomato pressed lightly into the purée, and arrange some walnut halves in a line down the centre — a tomato sauce goes well with it too.

SOYA WIENER SCHNITZEL

Imperial (Metric)	American
2 oz (55g) soya 'meat' slices	½ cupful soy 'meat' slices
1 oz (30g) wholemeal flour	¼ cupful wholewheat flour
Good pinch of mixed herbs	Good pinch of mixed herbs
Celery or onion salt	Celery or onion salt
Freshly ground black pepper	Freshly ground black pepper
½ tablespoonful vegetable oil	½ tablespoonful vegetable oil
½ oz (15g) vegan margarine	1 tablespoonful vegan margarine
Lemon wedges to serve	Lemon wedges to serve

1. Soak the slices in cold water for 15 minutes, then bring to the boil and cook for a minute only. Remove from the heat, drain, and leave to cool slightly.

2. Mix together the flour, herbs, salt and pepper, being generous with the flavourings.

3. Coat the slices with the flour mixture. In a frying pan (skillet) heat the oil with the margarine, drop in the slices one at a time, and fry for about 3 minutes on each side over a fairly high heat, then 5 minutes more with the heat turned down. (Fry the slices in oil only, if you prefer, though the combination of oil and margarine does give a better flavour).

4. Drain on paper towels and serve hot with lemon wedges.

Note: You can buy ready-mixed coating to save time. When buying the soya 'meat' slices, try to choose a pack that contains larger slices, as these work best in this particular recipe. As they are dried, and may have been roughly handled, they are sometimes broken, and though these pieces can be used in a casserole or sauce recipe, they do not look as attractive as the larger slices.

TOFU WIENER SCHNITZEL

You can use tofu in exactly the same way. Drain about 3 oz/85g (½ cupful) in a tea towel, pressing gently but firmly so that all the moisture is removed but the tofu is not broken. Cut it into thin slices, coat as above, and deep fry in hot vegetable oil for about 5 minutes, until golden brown. Drain, then serve with lemon wedges.

Note: Either of these recipes are ideal if you want a simple and quick protein to eat with potatoes and two vegetables when the family, for example, are having a steak or chops.

7

SWEET HARMONY

Gone are the days when vegetarianism was another word for stringent self-denial. No wine, no late nights — and no fancy foods whatsoever. Now everyone knows a little of what you fancy does you good. And if you feel a meal isn't complete without a sweet finale, there is no reason at all why you shouldn't have one.

Desserts can be simple or exotic, light or filling, thrifty or costly. And if you are really smart you will make your dessert not just an addition, but a valuable part of the meal. By using wholewheat flour, raw sugar, fresh and dried fruits, nuts and cream you can make them as nutritious as they are delicious.

So if you have a simple snack for your first course, maybe short on protein, you can balance it with a protein-rich dessert. After a stodgy dish, a fruit compote goes down a treat. Yogurt is especially delectable when you make it yourself and add real fruit (not that over-sweet synthetic kind you find in most mass-produced yogurts). Get used to eating these Real Food desserts and you will never be able to face an instant whip again. (The rest of your family will love them, too.)

APPLE PURÉE

Imperial (Metric)	American
A little water	A little water
1 lb (455g) cooking apples	1 pound cooking apples
Lemon rind, orange rind, cinnamon stick or clove	Lemon rind, orange rind, cinnamon stick or clove
3 oz (85g) honey	¼ cupful honey

1. Wet the bottom of a pan. Wash and stalk the apples, then cut them in pieces, add to the pan with the flavouring and dribble honey on top.

2. Heat till the apples collapse. Sieve, and eat hot or cold. Keeps well in an airtight container in the fridge.

DANISH APPLE PUDDING

Imperial (Metric)	American
6 oz (170g) fresh wholemeal breadcrumbs	3 cupsful wholewheat breadcrumbs
2 oz (55g) polyunsaturated margarine	¼ cupful polyunsaturated margarine
2 oz (55g) raw cane sugar	⅓ cupful raw cane sugar
1 lb (455g) Apple Purée (see above)	1 pound Apple Purée (see above)
Whipped cream, nuts, chocolate (optional)	Whipped cream, nuts, chocolate (optional)

1. Fry the breadcrumbs in the margarine till crisp, then add the sugar and stir till well mixed.

2. In a large dish alternate layers of purée and breadcrumbs, finishing with purée.

3. Cover or decorate with whipped cream and grated nuts or plain chocolate.

STUFFED BAKED APPLES

Imperial (Metric)	American
2 medium apples	2 medium apples
Approx. 2 teaspoonsful tahini	Approx. 2 teaspoonsful tahini
Approx. 2 teaspoonsful honey	Approx. 2 teaspoonsful honey
1 oz (30g) rolled oats	¼ cupful rolled oats
½ oz (15g) sultanas	1 tablespoonful golden seedless raisins
½ oz (15g) roasted hazelnuts	1 tablespoonful roasted hazelnuts

1. Wash, dry and remove the centre core from each apple, leaving a little of the apple in place at the bottom to form a base. Make a shallow slit around the centre of each apple to help prevent them splitting during cooking.

2. In a bowl combine the tahini and honey and then stir in the rolled oats, sultanas (golden seedless raisins) and chopped hazelnuts — if the mixture seems too dry add a little more tahini and honey. Use this mixture to stuff the apples, then stand them in a small ovenproof dish.

3. Bake at 375°F/190°C (Gas Mark 5) for about 40 minutes, or until the apples are tender.

4. Serve hot or cold, just as they are, or with custard, cream, yogurt — in fact, whatever you like!

Note: One apple is an average serving, so if no-one wants to share this dessert with you, keep the second apple in the fridge to eat cold another day.

YOGURT

Imperial (Metric)	American
1 pint (580ml) milk*	2½ cupsful milk*
1-2 tablespoonsful plain yogurt	1-2 tablespoonsful plain yogurt
Fruit flavouring (optional)	Fruit flavouring (optional)

1. Pour the milk into a saucepan that has a close fitting lid, and heat it to a temperature of 105°-115°F (40°-45°C), i.e. warm to the hand. Add the plain yogurt and mix well with the milk.

2. Replace the lid firmly, then wrap the saucepan in a towel and put in a warm place (e.g. an airing cupboard). The yogurt should set in 12-24 hours.

3. Add fresh fruit purée or any flavouring you fancy; or leave the yogurt plain and add honey and nuts when you wish to eat it. Keep your yogurt in the fridge, and it will stay fresh and tasty for some time.

*Use sterilized, skimmed, long life, soya or diluted evaporated milk.

BANANA COCONUT RAITA

Imperial (Metric)	American
1 medium banana	1 medium banana
Squeeze of lemon juice	Squeeze of lemon juice
¼ pint (140ml) plain yogurt	⅔ cupful plain yogurt
2 teaspoonsful raw cane sugar	2 teaspoonsful raw cane sugar
1 tablespoonful desiccated coconut, or to taste	1 tablespoonful desiccated coconut, or to taste
Pinch ground cardamom	Pinch ground cardamom

1. Slice the peeled banana into even-sized pieces and toss immediately in the lemon juice.

2. Stir all the ingredients together, and chill briefly before eating.

3. For a creamier dessert you can mash the bananas rather than chop them, then beat the pulp together with the other ingredients.

Note: Raitas are traditionally served as side dishes with a savoury such as curry, but they taste good at the end of the meal too. Try this one both ways, reducing the sugar by half when serving it as a side dish rather than a dessert.

BAKED EGG CUSTARD

Imperial (Metric)	American
2 eggs	2 eggs
Pinch of sea salt	Pinch of sea salt
1 oz (30g) raw cane sugar	2 tablespoonsful raw cane sugar
½ pint (285ml) milk	1⅓ cupsful milk
Grated nutmeg	Grated nutmeg

1. Beat the eggs together lightly, add the salt and sugar. Stir in the warmed (but not boiling) milk and continue stirring until the sugar is completely dissolved.

2. Pour the mixture into a small greased ovenproof dish, sprinkle with nutmeg, and stand this in another dish of cold water. (Alternatively you can divide it between 2 individual cups.)

3. Bake the custard at 300°F/150°C (Gas Mark 2) for about an hour, or until set firm.

Note: This makes two portions. Instead of nutmeg, try topping them when cooked with apple purée or jam.

PEAR CRUNCH
Serves 2

Imperial (Metric)	American
2 medium ripe pears	2 medium ripe pears
1 teaspoonful lemon juice	1 teaspoonful lemon juice
½ teaspoonful grated lemon peel	½ teaspoonful grated lemon peel
1 teaspoonful honey	1 teaspoonful honey
Pinch of mixed spices	Pinch of mixed spices
1 oz (30g) Crunchy Granola (see page 14)	2 tablespoonsful Crunchy Granola (see page 14)
½ oz (15g) walnuts	1 tablespoonful English walnuts
3 or 4 dates	3 or 4 dates

1. Peel, core and slice the pears as evenly as possible. Arrange them in an ovenproof dish.

2. Mix together the lemon juice, peel, honey and spices — you may
    need to warm the honey first. Spoon the mixture over the pears.
    Mix the granola with the chopped walnuts and dates, and sprinkle
    the mixture over the pears.

3. Bake at 350°F/180°C (Gas Mark 4) for about 30 minutes.

4. Serve warm or cold. Yogurt or cream makes a nice topping.

Note: Fresh peaches, cut in half and then treated the same way, make
a 'special occasion' version of this dessert dish.

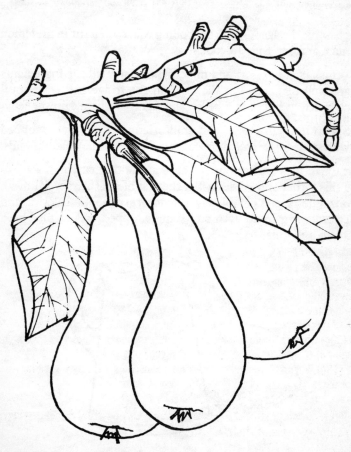

LEMON MOUSSE

Imperial (Metric)
1 packet lemon flavoured agar-agar
   jelly
4 tablespoonsful water
2 tablespoonsful lemon juice
½ pint (285ml) natural yogurt
½ pint (285ml) milk
Raw sugar chocolate
A few blanched almonds

American
1 packet lemon flavoured agar-agar
   jelly
⅓ cupful water
2 tablespoonsful lemon juice
1⅓ cupsful natural yogurt
1⅓ cupsful milk
Raw sugar chocolate
A few blanched almonds

1. Dissolve the agar-agar in the boiling water, then stir in the lemon juice and set aside to cool.

2. Whisk in the yogurt and milk, making sure all the ingredients are well blended. Put the bowl in the fridge and leave until completely set, then whisk again lightly to break up the jelly.

3. Spoon into tall glasses and chill briefly before serving topped with some finely grated chocolate or chopped blanched almonds.

Note: Quantities are for four on the assumption that you'll want to serve this rather special dessert at the end of a rather special meal. If your guests are completely unconcerned about calories and cholesterol, you could even add some whipped cream, plus both chocolate *and* nuts!

ALMOND ICE CREAM

Serves 4

Imperial (Metric)
½ pint (285ml) whipping cream
1 oz (30g) roasted almonds
2 oz (55g) raw cane sugar,
  powdered in grinder
Few drops almond extract
Few drops vanilla extract
2 egg whites

American
1⅓ cupsful whipping cream
¼ cupful roasted almonds
⅓ cupful raw cane sugar, powdered
  in grinder
Few drops almond extract
Few drops vanilla extract
2 egg whites

1. In a bowl whip the cream until light and smooth.

2. Grind the nuts and mix them with the sugar, then stir into the whipped cream.

3. Add the almond and vanilla extracts.

4. Whisk the egg whites and fold them into the other ingredients.

5. Pour the mixture into freezing trays and place in a freezer, with the controls on the lowest setting. Freeze it until firm, then tip into a bowl and whip to add air and break up the crystals. Return to the freezing tray and freeze again until firm.

Note: If you do not intend to eat the ice cream all at once, you could freeze it in individual containers and then just remove one serving from the freezer a short time before you need it.

SHORTCRUST PASTRY
(For Fruit Pies)

Imperial (Metric)	American
½ lb (225g) plain wholemeal flour	2 cupsful plain wholewheat flour
2 teaspoonsful baking powder	2 teaspoonsful baking soda
Pinch of sea salt	Pinch of sea salt
4 oz (115g) polyunsaturated margarine	½ cupful polyunsaturated margarine
Cold water	Cold water

1. Sieve the flour, baking powder and salt together in a bowl, adding any bran that is left in the sieve. Rub the fat into the flour until it looks like breadcrumbs.

2. Use the water to bind the mixture together — about two tablespoonsful should be enough.

3. Knead lightly to form a stiff dough, roll out fairly thinly on a floured board and use as a base or topping for fruit flans or pies.

4. This is sufficient to cover an 8 in. (20cm) dish, or, when used as a base and topping, will make one generous individual portion. Cooking time varies according to what goes into the pie, but as a guide — bake for 15 minutes at 400°F/200°C (Gas Mark 6) and then reduce for a further 30 minutes to 350°F/180°C (Gas Mark 4).

FRUIT CRUMBLE
Use the same recipe as for short crust pastry but do not add water. Simply sprinkle the breadcrumb-like mixture over the fruit, top with approximately 2 ounces (55g) raw cane sugar, and cook for 30 minutes at 350°F/180°C (Gas Mark 4).

FRUIT FLAN
Serves 4

Imperial (Metric)	**American**
Fresh or tinned fruit	Fresh or canned fruit
Prebaked flan case (see recipe page 78)	Prebaked flan case (see recipe page 78)
½ pint (285ml) fruit juice	1⅓ cupsful fruit juice
½ teaspoonful agar-agar	½ teaspoonful agar-agar
Raw cane sugar (optional)	Raw cane sugar (optional)

1. You can use fresh fruit in season, such as strawberries or gooseberries; tinned fruit such as mandarin oranges; or a mixture of fresh and tinned fruits. Place fruit evenly in the flan case making sure it is well filled.

2. Heat the juice and whisk in the agar-agar a little at a time so that it dissolves completely. Add a little sugar if you feel the fruit needs sweetening.

3. Cool slightly and pour carefully over the fruit. When cold, decorate with cream and/or nuts.

Note: This simple but impressive flan is ideal to serve to guests. In the unlikely event that any is left over, it will keep for a day or two.

ZABAGLIONE

Imperial (Metric)	American
1 egg	1 egg
1 tablespoonful soft light raw cane sugar	1 tablespoonful soft light raw cane sugar
1 tablespoonful marsala or brandy	1 tablespoonful marsala or brandy

1. Separate the egg. Whisk together the egg yolk and sugar over a pan of hot water (not boiling).

2. When it reaches a creamy consistency, add the marsala or brandy and whisk until thick and fluffy.

3. Remove from heat and fold in the whisked egg white; pour into a glass and eat straight away.

Note: This popular dessert goes down well with most people, so if you want to make it for your family just increase the quantities accordingly — treble this amount should be ample for 4 servings.

BREAD PUDDING
Serves 4

Imperial (Metric)	American
½ lb (225g) stale wholemeal bread	4 cupsful stale wholewheat bread
4 oz (115g) currants, raisins, sultanas (or mixture)	4 oz (115g) currants, raisins, golden seedless raisins (or mixture)
2 oz (55g) raw cane sugar	⅓ cupful raw cane sugar
2 oz (55g) butter	¼ cupful butter
1 oz (30g) chopped peel	2 tablespoonsful chopped peel
1 heaped teaspoonful mixed spice	1 heaped teaspoonful mixed spice
1 egg	1 egg
A little milk	A little milk

1. Break the bread into small pieces and soak for at least 30 minutes in cold water. Strain and squeeze it as dry as possible. Put in a basin and beat out lumps with a fork.

2. Add all ingredients except last two and beat well, then add egg and enough milk to bring mixture to a soft dropping consistency.

3. Put into a greased tin, preferably shallow, and bake at 350°F/180°C (Gas Mark 4) for about an hour.

4. When cooked, sprinkle with sugar and eat either hot with custard or cold as a kind of cake.

DATE AND APRICOT FRUITARIAN CAKES

Imperial (Metric)	American
3 oz (85g) dates	½ cupful dates
3 oz (85g) dried apricots	½ cupful dried apricots
1 oz (30g) ground cashew nuts	¼ cupful ground cashew nuts
½ oz (15g) sunflower seeds	1 tablespoonful sunflower seeds
Millet flakes or desiccated coconut	Millet flakes or desiccated coconut

1. Wash and chop the dried fruit and then mash well with the ground cashews. Stir in the sunflower seeds, mixing thoroughly.

2. Form into flat cakes and roll in millet flakes or desiccated coconut. For easier-to-handle cake you could place the dried fruit mix between sheets of rice paper.

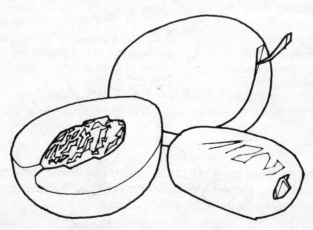

FRUIT AND NUT BALLS

Imperial (Metric)	American
6 oz (170g) dates	1 cupful dates
3 oz (85g) currants	½ cupful currants
1 teaspoonful powdered coriander	1 teaspoonful powdered coriander
2 oz (55g) ground hazelnuts	½ cupful ground hazelnuts
1 oz (30g) broken cashews	¼ cupful broken cashews
Juice ½ lemon	Juice ½ lemon

1. Wash the dried fruit; chop and mash the dates.

2. Add the coriander to the hazelnuts, then blend all the ingredients together.

3. Form into balls and roll in extra ground hazelnuts, or flatten the mixture into thin cakes and sandwich in rice paper.

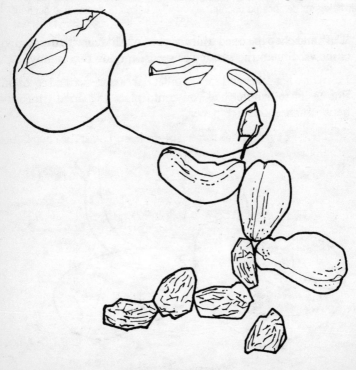

CHOCOLATE JELLY
Serves 2 or 3

Imperial (Metric)
1 pint (570ml) milk
1 heaped teaspoonful agar-agar
2 tablespoonsful raw cane sugar
1 heaped tablespoonful cocoa
Walnuts, chocolate nibs and cream
 to decorate (optional)

American
2½ cupsful milk
1 heaped teaspoonful agar-agar
2 tablespoonsful raw cane sugar
1 heaped tablespoonful cocoa
English walnuts, chocolate nibs and
 cream to decorate (optional)

1. Put milk in saucepan over low heat and bring to the boil. Sprinkle agar-agar onto milk a little at a time, and stir until it dissolves completely, then bring back to the boil and simmer for a few minutes.

2. Add sugar and cocoa and whisk well together. Pour into a dish, or small individual dishes, and leave in a cool place to set.

3. Decorate with chopped walnuts or chocolate nibs and cream for an especially scrumptious dessert. This makes two to three good servings so if no one wants to share it with you, save some for the next day.

Variation:
For fruit jelly use fruit juice instead of milk, and omit the cocoa. Add sugar or honey to taste.

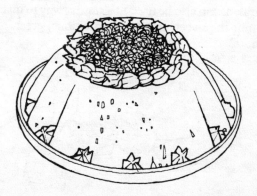

PUMPKIN PIE

Imperial (Metric)	American
3 lb (1½ kilos) pumpkin	3 pounds pumpkin
Vegetable oil	Vegetable oil
1 egg yolk	1 egg yolk
½ teaspoonful sea salt	½ teaspoonful sea salt
Honey	Honey
Cinnamon, nutmeg, allspice, cloves to taste	Cinnamon, nutmeg, allspice, cloves to taste
1 egg white	1 egg white
Pre-baked pastry base (see page 78)	Pre-baked pastry base (see page 78)
2 oz (55g) mixed nuts (optional)	½ cupful mixed nuts (optional)
Whipped cream (optional)	Whipped cream (optional)

1. Cut the pumpkin into chunks and sauté it in the oil, then cover pan and cook gently until it can be mashed into a purée. Add the egg yolk, salt, honey and spices and mix thoroughly — if possible in a blender.

2. Beat the egg white until stiff and fold it into the pumpkin mixture. Turn it all into a pre-baked pastry base, decorate with a sprinkling of nuts (and raisins, if you wish).

3. Bake for 15-20 minutes at 350°F/180°C (Gas Mark 4). Serve hot with whipped cream. It tastes good cold, too. So if any is left over keep it in the fridge for tomorrow.

Note: Pumpkins can also be used in a similar way to make a savoury pie. Just omit the sweetening and add onions, green peppers and chopped nuts.

8.
A BAKER'S DOZEN

One upon a time the smell of bread baking in the oven was to be found in every home. In recent years most bread has come fresh from the waxpaper rather than the oven. But there is a swing back to home baking — to making real bread that is warm to touch, satisfyingly chewy to eat, and full of goodness. The kind of food, in fact, that earned bread the title Staff of Life. And with this swing has come a renewed interest in baking muffins, cakes, biscuits, and many more good things.

Baking isn't, of course, restricted to vegetarians. But the recipes given here are all special in that none of them are empty foods based on taste value alone, as are so many recipes. All of them are made from wholesome ingredients so that what tastes good also does you good.

When baking for one it is wise to bake items that keep well (or be prepared to put on weight!). If you have a freezer you can bake bigger batches of bread, cakes and biscuits, wrap them in silver foil, and freeze them. They will keep fresh for weeks — providing the rest of the family don't discover how delicious they are!

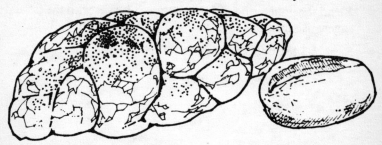

Breads

QUICK WHOLEMEAL BREAD

Imperial (Metric)	American
1 oz (30g) fresh yeast *or* ½ oz (15g) dried yeast	2½ tablespoonsful fresh yeast *or* 1 tablespoonful dried yeast
½ pint (285ml) warm water	1⅓ cupsful warm water
1 teaspoonful sea salt	1 teaspoonful sea salt
1 lb (455g) wholemeal flour	4 cupsful wholewheat flour
1 teaspoonful vegetable oil	1 teaspoonful vegetable oil

1. In a small bowl cream the yeast with a little of the water, and set aside.

2. In a large warmed bowl mix the salt with the flour. When the yeast begins to bubble stir it, with the oil, into the flour, then add most of the remaining water.

3. Mix well, adding more water if necessary, and knead the dough until it has an elastic consistency. Place in a warmed tin and leave to rise for about 15 minutes.

4. Bake for about 45 minutes at 400°F/200°C (Gas Mark 6).

Variations:
- Omit 1 oz/30g (4 tablespoonsful) flour and replace it with 1 oz/30g (4 tablespoonsful) carob powder.

- Blend the grated rind of 1-2 lemons or oranges with the fat and sugar, use medium eggs and add 1 tablespoonful fruit juice.

- Sieve 2-3 teaspoonsful instant coffee with the flour.

TEA BISCUITS

Imperial (Metric)
4 oz (115g) polyunsaturated
margarine
½ lb (225g) wholemeal flour
⅓ teaspoonful bicarbonate of soda
½ level teaspoonful cream of tartar
3 oz (85g) raw cane sugar

American
½ cupful polyunsaturated margarine
2 cupsful wholewheat flour
⅓ teaspoonful baking soda
½ level teaspoonful cream of tartar
⅔ cupful raw cane sugar

1. Rub the fat into the dry ingredients and add just enough water to make a stiff paste.

2. Form into a roll about 2 in. (5cm) in diameter. Cut into ¼ in. (½cm) thick slices.

3. Bake for 15 minutes at 400°F/200°C (Gas Mark 6) until just changing colour.

4. Cool biscuits and store them in a tin or airtight container.

Variations:
- Add 2 teaspoonsful molasses or treacle.
- Add 1 teaspoonful mixed spice.
- Add ½ teaspoonful caraway seeds.
- Add 1 teaspoonful ground ginger.

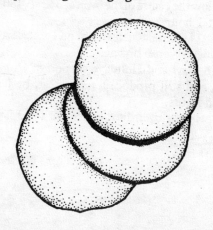

HONEY CAKE

Imperial (Metric)	American
½ lb (225g) plain wholemeal flour	2 cupsful wholewheat flour
Pinch of sea salt	Pinch of sea salt
1 teaspoonful baking powder	1 teaspoonful baking powder
1 teaspoonful mixed spice	1 teaspoonful mixed spice
½ lb (225g) thin honey	¾ cupful thin honey
½ pint (285ml) milk	1⅓ cupsful milk
1 oz (30g) butter	2½ tablespoonsful butter
4 oz (115g) raw cane sugar	½ cupful raw cane sugar
2 oz (55g) glacé cheries	⅓ cupful glacé cherries
2 oz (55g) chopped peel	⅓ cupful chopped peel
Grated rind of a lemon	Grated rind of a lemon
2 oz (55g) flaked almonds	½ cupful slivered almonds

1. Sieve the flour, salt, baking powder and spice into a bowl.

2. Pour the honey into a saucepan, add the milk and butter, and heat gently until blended. Sitr on to the flour and beat well.

3. Mix together the sugar, cherries, peel and lemon rind, and add to the rest of the ingredients, making sure they are evenly distributed. Put the mixture into a greased and lined loaf tin (or round cake tin) and sprinkle with the almonds.

4. Bake just below the centre of the oven at 350°F/180°C (Gas Mark 4) for about 1 hour.

Variation:
This is the High-Days-and-Holidays version of Honey Cake. You can economize, and still produce a tasty treat, by leaving out the cherries, peel and nuts.

BRAN MUFFINS
Makes 12 large muffins

Imperial (Metric)	American
6 oz (170g) plain wholemeal flour	1½ cupsful plain wholewheat flour
Pinch of sea salt	Pinch of sea salt
4½ teaspoonsful baking powder	4½ teaspoonsful baking powder
3 oz (85g) raw cane sugar	⅓ cupful raw cane sugar
6 oz (17g) *All-Bran*	1 cupful *All-Bran*
⅔ pint (340ml) milk	1½ cupsful milk
1½ oz (40g) melted polyunsaturated margarine	3½ tablespoonsful melted polyunsaturated margarine
2 eggs, beaten	2 eggs, beaten
2 oz (55g) broken walnuts	½ cupful broken English walnuts

1. Sift the flour with the salt and baking powder, add the sugar.

2. Cover bran with milk and leave to soak for 5 minutes. Add melted margarine and beaten eggs to bran mixture, then stir it all into the flour. Beat very thoroughly. Add the nuts.

3. Fill ready-greased patty tins to the top and bake at 425°F/220°C (Gas Mark 7) for 20-25 minutes, or until well risen.

Variation:

Muffins can be made more nutritious by the addition of a little soya flour, wheatgerm or extra skimmed milk powder. You can vary the taste by using different kinds of nuts and/or seeds; adding currants, raisins or dates; by substituting honey for the sugar. Add some rolled oats for especially crunchy muffins. Use less sweetener and you can eat muffins as a kind of bread with soup or salad. And if they get a little stale, simply slice them, toast them, and top with honey or peanut butter. Delicious!

FLAPJACKS
Makes 6-8

Imperial (Metric)	American
2 oz (55g) polyunsaturated margarine or butter	¼ cupful of polyunsaturated margarine or butter
1 oz (30g) raw cane sugar	2 tablespoonsful raw cane sugar
1 oz (30g) honey or syrup	1 tablespoonful honey or syrup
4 oz (115g) rolled oats	1 cupful rolled oats
Pinch of sea salt	Pinch of sea salt

1. Grease a 7 in. (18cm) sandwich tin. Heat the margarine or butter in a small saucepan, stir in the sugar and honey then add the rolled oats and salt. Mix thoroughly.

2. Press the mixture into the tin and bake in the centre of the oven at 375°F/190°C (Gas Mark 5) until firm to the touch. This should take 20-30 minutes, but check after 15 minutes and if the flapjacks seem too brown, lower the heat for the rest of the time.

3. Mark into fingers when still hot but do not remove them from the tin until completely cold.

TEA CAKES
Makes 20

Imperial (Metric)	**American**
½ lb (225g) self-raising wholemeal flour	2 cupsful self-raising wholewheat flour
Pinch of sea salt	Pinch of sea salt
1 teaspoonful baking powder	1 teaspoonful baking powder
1 tablespoonful warm water	1 tablespoonful warm water
6 oz (170g) polyunsaturated margarine	⅔ cupful polyunsaturated margarine
6 oz (170g) raw cane sugar	1 cupful raw cane sugar
3 beaten eggs	3 beaten eggs

1. Sift the flour with the salt and baking powder, then add all the remaining ingredients and mix very thoroughly. Two-thirds fill some deep patty tins with the mixture (greasing them first if they are not non-stick).

2. Bake at 425°F/220°C (Gas Mark 7) for 20-30 minutes when cakes should have risen and turned golden brown.

Variations:
This basic recipe can be adapted in a large number of ways.
- Add nuts and dates.
- Add apple purée and cinnamon.
- Add some chopped glacé cherries and/or chopped peel.
- Omit 1 oz/30g (4 tablespoonsful) of flour and replace with 1 oz/30g (4 tablespoonsful) carob powder.
- Add raisins and 2 tablespoonsful marmalade.
- Replace sugar with honey and add some grated lemon rind.

DATE SCONES
Makes 8

Imperial (Metric)	American
½ lb (225g) plain wholemeal flour	2 cupsful plain wholewheat flour
Pinch of sea salt	Pinch of sea salt
1 teaspoonful baking powder	1 teaspoonful baking powder
1 oz (30g) butter or polyunsaturated margarine	2½ tablespoonsful butter or polyunsaturated margarine
1 oz (30g) raw cane sugar	2 tablespoonsful raw cane sugar
2 oz (55g) chopped dates	⅓ cupful chopped dates
Milk to mix	Milk to mix

1. Sieve flour, salt and baking powder into a bowl, adding any bran that is left in the sieve.

2. Rub in the butter or margarine, add the sugar and finely chopped dates.

3. Mix to a soft rolling consistency with the milk, knead the dough, then roll out to ½-¾ in. (1-1.5cm) thickness and cut into rounds with a cup.

4. Place on a greased baking sheet and bake at the top of the oven at 425°F/220°C (Gas Mark 7) for about 20 minutes. Scones are cooked when firm to touch.

Variations:
● Add 2 oz/55g (⅓ cupful) sultanas (golden seedless raisins) instead of dates.
● Add 2 oz/55g (⅓ cupful) glacé cherries instead of dates.
● Add 1-2 tablespoonsful molasses to the dough before the milk is added — omit the dates and sugar.

LUNCHEON CAKE

Imperial (Metric)
12 oz (340g) wholemeal flour
1 oz (30g) soya flour
1 teaspoonful mixed spice
½ teaspoonful bicarbonate of soda
¾ teaspoonful cream of tartar
6 oz (170g) raw cane sugar
6 oz (170g) polyunsaturated
  margarine
½ lb (225g) currants and sultanas
  (any proportion)
1 oz (30g) chopped peel
1 tablespoonful lemon juice
1 tablespoonful honey or treacle
Cold water to mix

American
3 cupsful wholewheat flour
¼ cupful soy flour
1 teaspoonful mixed spice
½ teaspoonful baking soda
¾ teaspoonful cream of tartar
1 cupful raw cane sugar
¾ cupful polyunsaturated margarine
1¼ cupsful currants and golden
  seedless raisins (any proportion)
2½ tablespoonsful chopped peel
1 tablespoonful lemon juice
1 tablespoonful honey or treacle
Cold water to mix

1. Mix the dry ingredients, then rub in the fat. Add the fruit, lemon juice, honey and sufficient cold water to make the mixture easy to beat. Do so until it is pale and light in texture.

2. Put the mixture into a flat greased tin lined with greased paper and bake for 45 minutes at 400°F/200°C (Gas Mark 6). Allow the cake to cool before turning out of the tin.

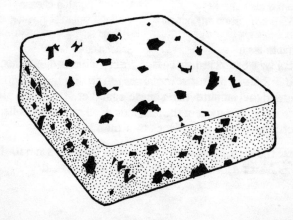

CHEDDAR CHEESE BISCUITS

Version 1:

Imperial (Metric)

3 oz (85g) polyunsaturated margarine or butter
6 oz (170g) plain wholemeal flour
Seasoning to taste
4 oz (115g) grated cheese
2-3 teaspoonsful yeast extract
6 tablespoonsful water

American

⅓ cupful polyunsaturated margarine or butter
1½ cupful plain wholewheat flour
Seasoning to taste
1 cupful grated cheese
2-3 teaspoonsful yeast extract
½ cupful water

1. Rub the fat into the flour, season, mix with the grated cheese. Dissolve the yeast extract in some of the water and add to the mixture to bind it.

2. Roll out the dough to about ¼ in. (5mm) thickness then cut into rounds either with a knife, a cup, or a cutter. Bake the biscuits on a tray for about 30 minutes at 350°F/180°C (Gas Mark 4).

Version 2:

Imperial (Metric)

3 oz (85g) polyunsaturated margarine or butter
2 oz (55g) grated cheese
4 oz (115g) self-raising wholemeal flour
Seasoning to taste
2 oz (55g) flaked, blanched almonds

American

⅓ cupful polyunsaturated margarine or butter
½ cupful grated cheese
1 cupful self-raising wholewheat flour
Seasoning to taste
½ cupful slivered, blanched almonds

1. Cream the fat and the cheese together, then add the flour, seasoning, and most of the almonds. Roll into small balls, topping each one with a few pieces of almonds.

2. Bake the biscuits on a tray for about 15 minutes at 350°F/180°C (Gas Mark 4). Allow room for them to spread.

9.

MATCH-MAKER MEALS

When the family are having:	You can have:
For breakfast	
Cereals	The same cereals or muesli, granola, other wholegrain cereals.
Fried egg, bacon, kidneys, etc.	The same, but omit the meat and fry in vegetable oil.
Toasted bacon sandwich	Eggs, beans, mushrooms, etc., on toast.
For a light meal	
Soups — chicken, consomme, Scotch broth	Vegetable soup (keep your own instant soups in a separate cupboard).
Pea soup with chopped ham	If you don't want to just miss the ham, add soya 'meat' chunks.
Grilled or fried fish cakes, fish fingers, sausages, rissoles	Grilled or fried fritters with the same vegetables as everyone else.
Ham omelette	Omelette with vegetarian filling.
Cold meat with hot vegetables	Tinned nut 'meat' or cold vegetarian savoury with vegetables.

Spaghetti bolognese	Spaghetti with soya 'meat' sauce.
Meat curry with rice	Egg, fruit, vegetable, soya 'meat' curry with rice.
Sausages and mashed potatoes	Tinned 'sausages' from your health food store.
Fish and chips	Fried egg or fritters and chips.
Liver, bacon and vegetables	A vegetable/nut dish.
Pancakes (crêpes) with a meat-savoury filling	Pancakes (crêpes) with vegetables, cheese and/or nuts.

For a main meal

Any slow roasting meat, i.e. beef, lamb, mutton, pork, veal	Grain casserole Flan A bean or rice loaf 'Meat' stew Stuffed vegetables Jacket potatoes with various toppings Oven-cooked macaroni or lasagne.
Any medium-quick roasting dish, i.e. chicken, turkey, duck, halibut, sole, fish pie, hot-pot, stews, moussaka	Bean casserole Vegetarian moussaka If you are using a stuffing with the meat, such as a rice/nut mix, cook some of it separately wrapped in silver foil, and eat with the vegetables.
Any quick-roasting meat, i.e. pies such as chicken and ham, steak and kidney; sausage rolls; pigeon; rabbit	Soufflé Vegetable casserole Sausage rolls made with soya 'meat' or vegetable filling.

Pizza	If the family want meat on their pizza, mark your portion and top it with everything except the meat.
Shepherd's Pie	Shepherd's Pie made with soya minced 'meat' or a lentil savoury.
Fried chicken, corn fritters, vegetables	Corn fritters (add some soya flour and a high protein sauce) and vegetables.
Toad-in-the-hole (or chops cooked the same way)	Use the same batter to make your own individual portion, pouring it over tomatoes and mushrooms instead of meat.
Boiled bacon, pease pudding, carrots, onion	Pease pudding (made with eggs) and vegetables.
Risotto	Remove your portion of rice before meat is added and add your choice of nuts, cheese, seeds, vegetables.
Grilled chops and vegetables	Eat the vegetables with a high-protein sauce (choose one that can be served over the chops, too).

INDEX